CROCK·POT®
◆ THE ORIGINAL SLOW COOKER ◆

3 Books in 1

•5 Ingredients or less

•Chicken

•Soups & Stews

Scalloped Potatoes & Ham
(page 26)

Forty-Clove Chicken
(page 98)

Beggar's Chowder
(page 166)

Publications International, Ltd.

Pictured on the front cover (left to right): Scalloped Potatoes & Ham (page 26), Forty-Clove Chicken (page 98) and Beggar's Chowder (page 166).

Pictured on the back cover (left to right): Easy Dirty Rice (page 60) and My Mother's Sausage and Vegetable Soup (page 162).

ISBN: 978-1-68022-032-2

Library of Congress Control Number: 2008929847

Manufactured in China.

8 7 6 5 4 3 2 1

Introduction

Sizes of CROCK-POT® Slow Cookers

Smaller **CROCK-POT®** slow cookers—such as 1- to 3½-quart models—are the perfect size for cooking for singles, a couple or empty nesters (and also for serving dips).

While medium-size **CROCK-POT®** slow cookers (those holding somewhere between 3 quarts and 5 quarts) will easily cook enough food at a time to feed a small family. They are also convenient for holiday side dishes or appetizers.

Large **CROCK-POT®** slow cookers are great for large family dinners, holiday entertaining and potluck suppers. A 6- to 7-quart model is ideal if you like to make meals in advance, or have dinner tonight and store leftovers for another day.

Types of CROCK-POT® Slow Cookers

Current **CROCK-POT®** slow cookers come equipped with many different features and benefits, from auto cook programs to oven-safe stoneware to timed programming. Please visit www.crock-pot.com to find the **CROCK-POT®** slow cooker that best suits your needs.

How you plan to use a **CROCK-POT®** slow cooker may affect the model you choose to purchase. For everyday cooking, choose a size large enough to serve your family. If you plan to use the **CROCK-POT®** slow cooker primarily for entertaining, choose one of the larger sizes. Basic **CROCK-POT®** slow cookers can hold as little as 16 ounces or as much as 7 quarts. The smallest sizes are great for keeping dips warm on a buffet, while the larger sizes can more readily fit large quantities of food and larger roasts.

Cooking, Stirring and Food Safety

CROCK-POT® slow cookers are safe to leave unattended. The outer heating base may get hot as it cooks, but it should not pose a fire hazard. The heating element in the heating base functions at a low wattage and is safe for your countertops.

Your **CROCK-POT®** slow cooker should be filled about one-half to three-fourths full for most recipes unless otherwise instructed. Lean meats such as chicken or pork tenderloin will cook faster than meats with more connective tissue and fat such as beef chuck or pork shoulder. Bone-in meats will take longer than boneless cuts. Typical **CROCK-POT®** slow cooker dishes take approximately 7 to 8 hours to reach the simmer point on LOW and about 3 to 4 hours on HIGH. Once the vegetables and meat start to simmer and braise, their flavors will fully blend and meat will become fall-off-the-bone tender.

According to the U.S. Department of Agriculture, all bacteria are killed at a temperature of 165°F. It's important to follow the recommended cooking times and not to open the lid often, especially early in the cooking process when heat is building up inside the unit. If you need to open the lid to check on your food or are adding additional ingredients, remember to allow additional cooking time if necessary to ensure food is cooked through and tender.

Large **CROCK-POT®** slow cookers, the 6- to 7-quart sizes, may benefit from a quick stir halfway through cook time to help distribute heat and promote even cooking. It's usually unnecessary to stir at all, as even ½ cup liquid will help to distribute heat and the stoneware is the perfect medium for holding food at an even temperature throughout the cooking process.

Oven-Safe Stoneware

All **CROCK-POT®** slow cooker removable stoneware inserts may (without their lids) be used safely in ovens at up to 400°F. In addition,

all **CROCK-POT®** slow cookers are microwavable without their lids. If you own another slow cooker brand, please refer to your owner's manual for specific stoneware cooking medium tolerances.

Frozen Food

Frozen food can be successfully cooked in a **CROCK-POT®** slow cooker. However, it will require longer cooking time than the same recipe made with fresh food. It is almost always preferable to thaw frozen food prior to placing it in the **CROCK-POT®** slow cooker. Using an instant-read thermometer is recommended to ensure meat is fully cooked through.

Pasta and Rice

If you are converting a recipe for a **CROCK-POT®** slow cooker that calls for uncooked pasta, first cook the pasta on the stovetop just until slightly tender. Then add the pasta to the **CROCK-POT®** slow cooker. If you are converting a recipe for the **CROCK-POT®** slow cooker that calls for cooked rice, stir in raw rice with the other recipe ingredients plus ¼ cup extra liquid per ¼ cup of raw rice.

Beans

Beans must be softened completely before combining with sugar and/or acidic foods in the **CROCK-POT®** slow cooker. Sugar and acid have a hardening effect on beans and will prevent softening. Fully cooked canned beans may be used as a substitute for dried beans.

Vegetables

Root vegetables often cook more slowly than meat. Cut vegetables accordingly to cook at the same rate as meat—large or small or lean versus marbled—and place near the sides or bottom of the stoneware to facilitate cooking.

Herbs

Fresh herbs add flavor and color when added at the end of the cooking cycle; if added at the beginning, many fresh herbs' flavor will dissipate over long cook times. Ground and/or dried herbs and spices work well in slow cooking and may be added at the beginning of cook time. For dishes with shorter cook times, hearty fresh herbs such as rosemary and thyme hold up well. The flavor power of all herbs and spices can vary greatly depending on their particular strength and shelf life. Use chili powders and garlic powder sparingly, as these can sometimes intensify over the long cook times. Always taste the finished dish and correct seasonings including salt and pepper.

Liquids

It's not necessary to use more than ½ to 1 cup liquid in most instances since juices in meats and vegetables are retained more in slow cooking than in conventional cooking. Excess liquid can be cooked down and concentrated after slow cooking on the stovetop or by removing meat and vegetables from stoneware, stirring in one of the following thickeners and setting the slow cooker to HIGH. Cover; cook on HIGH for approximately 15 minutes or until juices are thickened.

Flour: All-purpose flour is often used to thicken soups or stews. Stir cold water into the flour in a small bowl until smooth. With the **CROCK-POT®** slow cooker on HIGH, whisk the flour mixture into the liquid in the **CROCK-POT®** slow cooker. Cover; cook on HIGH 15 minutes or until the mixture is thickened.

Cornstarch: Cornstarch gives sauces a clear, shiny appearance; it's used most often for sweet dessert sauces and stir-fry sauces. Stir cold water into the cornstarch in a small bowl until the cornstarch dissolves. Quickly stir this mixture into the liquid in the **CROCK-POT®** slow cooker; the sauce will thicken as soon as the liquid simmers. Cornstarch breaks down with too much heat, so never add it at the beginning of the slow cooking process and turn off the heat as soon as the sauce thickens.

Arrowroot: Arrowroot (or arrowroot flour) comes from the root of a tropical plant that is dried and ground to a powder; it produces a thick clear sauce. Those who are allergic to wheat often use it in place of flour. Place arrowroot in a small bowl or cup and stir in cold water until the mixture is smooth. Quickly stir this mixture into the liquid in the **CROCK-POT®** slow cooker. Arrowroot thickens below the boiling point, so it even works well in a **CROCK-POT®** slow cooker on LOW. Too much stirring can break down an arrowroot mixture.

Tapioca: Tapioca is a starchy substance extracted from the root of the cassava plant. Its greatest advantage is that it withstands long cooking, making it an ideal choice for slow cooking. Add it at the beginning of cooking and you'll get a clear thickened sauce in the finished dish. Dishes using tapioca as a thickener are best cooked on the LOW setting; tapioca may become stringy when boiled for a long time.

Milk

Milk, cream and sour cream break down during extended cooking. When possible, add them during the last 15 to 30 minutes of slow cooking, until just heated through. Condensed soups may be substituted for milk and may cook for extended times.

Fish

Fish is delicate and should be stirred into the **CROCK-POT®** slow cooker gently during the last 15 to 30 minutes of cooking time. Cover; cook just until cooked through and serve immediately.

Baked Goods

If you wish to prepare bread, cakes or pudding cakes in a **CROCK-POT®** slow cooker, you may want to purchase a covered, vented metal cake pan accessory for your **CROCK-POT®** slow cooker. You can also use any straight-sided soufflé dish or deep cake pan that will fit into the stoneware of your unit. Baked goods can be prepared directly in the stoneware; however, they can be a little difficult to remove from the insert, so follow the recipe directions carefully.

CROCK-POT® Slow Cooker Recipes with 5 Ingredients or Less

A well-stocked pantry is a shortcut to preparing dishes and entire meals efficiently. The first six chapters of this cookbook take full advantage of the kinds of everyday ingredients most cooks commonly have on hand. They feature recipes that can be created with 5 ingredients and/or the addition of these common pantry items:

- Water
- Milk
- Butter
- Vegetable oil
- Olive oil
- Salt and black pepper
- Other common spices (such as ground cinnamon, ground nutmeg, ground red pepper, red pepper flakes, garlic powder, ground cumin, ground oregano, dried thyme, chili powder, paprika, etc.)
- All-purpose flour
- Cornstarch
- Arrowroot
- Tapioca
- Granulated sugar

These slow-cooked recipes are perfect for busy days when you don't have time to make another stop at the grocery store.

5 Ingredients or Less

TABLE OF CONTENTS

Easy Beef Entrées

Best-Ever Roast

1 beef chuck shoulder roast (3 to 5 pounds)
1 can (10¾ ounces) condensed cream of mushroom soup, undiluted
1 envelope (1 ounce) dry onion soup mix
4 to 5 medium potatoes, quartered
4 cups baby carrots

1. Place roast in **CROCK-POT®** slow cooker. (If necessary, cut roast in half to fit into **CROCK-POT®** slow cooker.) Combine mushroom soup and onion soup mix in medium bowl. Pour over roast. Cover; cook on LOW 4 hours.

2. Add potatoes and carrots. Cover; cook on LOW 2 hours.

Makes 6 to 8 servings

Veggie Soup with Beef

2 cans (15 ounces each) mixed vegetables

1 pound beef stew meat

1 can (8 ounces) tomato sauce

2 cloves garlic, minced

Water

Place all ingredients in **CROCK-POT®** slow cooker. Add enough water to fill **CROCK-POT®** slow cooker to within ½ inch of top. Cover; cook on LOW 8 to 10 hours.

Makes 4 servings

Smothered Steak

4 to 6 beef cube steaks (about 1½ to 2 pounds)

All-purpose flour

1 can (10¾ ounces) condensed cream of mushroom soup, undiluted

1 package (1 ounce) dry onion soup mix

Hot cooked rice (optional)

1. Dust steaks lightly with flour. Place in **CROCK-POT®** slow cooker. Combine mushroom soup and onion soup mix in medium bowl. Pour over steak.

2. Cover; cook on LOW 6 to 8 hours. Serve over rice, if desired.

Makes 4 servings

Veggie Soup with Beef

Tavern Burger

2 **pounds ground beef**
½ **cup ketchup**
¼ **cup packed brown sugar**
¼ **cup prepared yellow mustard**
   Hamburger buns

1. Cook beef in medium skillet over medium-high heat until no longer pink, stirring to break up meat. Drain fat. Transfer beef to **CROCK-POT**® slow cooker.

2. Add ketchup, sugar and mustard to **CROCK-POT**® slow cooker; mix well. Cover; cook on LOW 4 to 6 hours. Serve on buns.

Makes 8 servings

Tip: Serve a scoopful on a hamburger bun. This is also known to some people as "BBQ's" or "loose-meat sandwiches." For added flavor, add a can of pork and beans when adding the other ingredients.

Dad's Dill Beef Roast

1 **beef chuck roast (3 to 4 pounds)**
1 **large jar whole dill pickles, undrained**

Place beef in **CROCK-POT**® slow cooker. Pour pickles with juice over top of beef. Cover; cook on LOW 8 to 10 hours. Remove beef to platter and shred with two forks.

Makes 6 to 8 servings

Serving Suggestion: Pile this beef onto toasted rolls or buns or, for an easy dinner variation, serve it with mashed potatoes.

Tavern Burger

Easy Beef Stew

2 **pounds beef stew meat, cut into 1-inch cubes**

1 **can (4 ounces) mushrooms**

1 **envelope (1 ounce) dry onion soup mix**

1 **can (10¾ ounces) condensed cream of mushroom soup, undiluted**

⅓ **cup red or white wine**

Hot cooked noodles (optional)

Combine beef, mushrooms, soup mix, soup and wine in **CROCK-POT®** slow cooker. Cover; cook on LOW 8 to 12 hours. Serve over noodles, if desired.

Makes 4 to 6 servings

Tip: Browning the beef before cooking it in the **CROCK-POT®** slow cooker isn't necessary, but helps to enhance the flavor and appearance of the stew. If you have the time, use nonstick cooking spray and brown the meat in a large skillet before placing it in the **CROCK-POT®** slow cooker; follow the recipe as written.

Swiss Steak Stew

2 to 3 boneless beef top sirloin steaks (about 4 pounds)

2 cans (about 14 ounces each) diced tomatoes, undrained

2 medium green bell peppers, cut into ½-inch strips

2 medium onions, chopped

1 tablespoon seasoned salt

1 teaspoon black pepper

Cut each steak into 3 to 4 pieces; place in **CROCK-POT®** slow cooker. Add tomatoes with juice, bell peppers and onions. Season with salt and pepper. Cover; cook on LOW 8 hours or until meat is tender.

Makes 10 servings

Easy Beef Sandwiches

1 large onion, sliced

1 boneless beef bottom round roast (about 3 to 5 pounds)

1 cup water

1 envelope (1 ounce) au jus gravy mix

French bread, sliced lengthwise

Provolone cheese (optional)

1. Place onion slices in bottom of **CROCK-POT®** slow cooker; top with roast. Combine water and gravy mix in small bowl; pour over roast. Cover and cook on LOW 7 to 9 hours.

2. Shred meat using two forks. Serve on French bread, topped with cheese, if desired. Serve cooking liquid on the side for dipping.

Makes 6 to 8 servings

Swiss Steak Stew

Easy Chili

1   **teaspoon vegetable oil**
1   **pound ground beef**
1   **medium onion, chopped**
2   **cans (10¾ ounces each) condensed tomato soup, undiluted**
1   **cup water**
    Salt and black pepper
    Chili powder

1. Heat oil in large skillet over medium-high heat. Add beef and onion. Cook and stir until beef is well browned. Drain excess fat.

2. Place meat mixture, soup and water in **CROCK-POT®** slow cooker. Add salt, pepper and chili powder to taste. Cover; cook on LOW 6 hours.

Makes 4 servings

Tip: This dish can cook up to 8 hours. Garnish with shredded cheese and serve with crackers or thick slices of Italian bread.

Bacon and Onion Brisket

6 slices bacon, cut crosswise into ½-inch strips

1 flat-cut boneless brisket (about 2½ pounds)

   Salt and black pepper

3 medium onions, sliced

2 cans (10¾ ounces each) condensed beef consommé, undiluted

1. Cook bacon strips in large skillet over medium-high heat about 3 minutes. Do not overcook. Transfer bacon with slotted spoon to **CROCK-POT®** slow cooker.

2. Season brisket with salt and pepper. Return skillet to medium-high heat and sear brisket in hot bacon fat on all sides, turning as it browns. Transfer to **CROCK-POT®** slow cooker.

3. Lower skillet heat to medium. Add sliced onions to skillet. Cook and stir 3 to 5 minutes or until softened. Add to **CROCK-POT®** slow cooker. Pour in consommé. Cover; cook on HIGH 6 to 8 hours or until meat is tender.

4. Transfer brisket to cutting board and let rest 10 minutes. Slice brisket against the grain into thin slices, and arrange on platter. Add salt and pepper, if desired. Spoon bacon, onions and cooking liquid over brisket to serve.

Makes 6 servings

Pork Dishes

Shredded Pork Wraps

- 1 **cup salsa, divided**
- 2 **tablespoons cornstarch**
- 1 **boneless pork loin roast (2 pounds)**
- 6 **(8-inch) flour tortillas**
- 3 **cups broccoli slaw mix**
- ½ **cup (2 ounces) shredded Cheddar cheese (optional)**

1. Combine ¼ cup salsa and cornstarch in small bowl; stir until smooth. Pour mixture into **CROCK-POT®** slow cooker. Top with pork roast. Pour remaining ¾ cup salsa over roast. Cover; cook on LOW 6 to 8 hours.

2. Transfer roast to cutting board. Trim and discard fat from pork. Pull pork into coarse shreds using 2 forks.

3. Divide shredded meat evenly among tortillas. Spoon about 2 tablespoons salsa mixture on top of meat in each tortilla. Top evenly with broccoli slaw and cheese, if desired. Fold bottom edge of tortilla over filling; fold in sides. Roll up completely to enclose filling. Serve remaining salsa mixture as dipping sauce.

Makes 6 servings

Steamed Pork Buns

½ **container (18 ounces) refrigerated shredded cooked pork in barbecue sauce***

1 **tablespoon Asian garlic chili sauce**

1 **container (about 16 ounces) large refrigerated biscuits (8 biscuits)**

Dipping Sauce (recipe follows)

Sliced green onions (optional)

*Look for pork in plain, not smoky, barbecue sauce.

1. Combine pork and chili sauce in medium bowl. Split biscuits in half. Roll or stretch each biscuit half into 4-inch circle. Spoon 1 tablespoon pork onto center of each bottom. Cover with biscuit top, gather edges around filling and press to seal.

2. Generously butter 2-quart baking dish that fits inside **CROCK-POT®** slow cooker. Arrange filled biscuits in single layer, overlapping slightly if necessary. Cover dish with buttered foil, buttered side down.

3. Place small rack in **CROCK-POT®** slow cooker. Add 1 inch hot water (water should not come to top of rack). Place baking dish on rack. Cover; cook on HIGH 2 hours.

4. Meanwhile, prepare Dipping Sauce. Garnish pork buns with green onions, if desired. Serve with Dipping Sauce.

Makes 8 servings

Dipping Sauce: Stir together 2 tablespoons rice vinegar, 2 tablespoons soy sauce, 4 teaspoons sugar and 1 teaspoon toasted sesame oil in a small bowl until sugar is dissolved.

Scalloped Potatoes & Ham

- 6 **large russet potatoes, sliced into ¼-inch rounds**
- 1 **ham steak (about 1½ pounds), cut into cubes**
- 1 **can (10¾ ounces) condensed cream of mushroom soup, undiluted**
- 1 **soup can water**
- 1 **cup (4 ounces) shredded Cheddar cheese**
- **Grill seasoning to taste**

1. Spray inside of **CROCK-POT®** slow cooker with nonstick cooking spray. Layer potatoes and ham in **CROCK-POT®** slow cooker.

2. In large mixing bowl, combine soup, water, cheese and seasoning; pour over potatoes and ham.

3. Cover; cook on HIGH about 3½ hours or until potatoes are fork-tender. Turn **CROCK-POT®** slow cooker to LOW and continue cooking about 1 hour or until done.

Makes 5 to 6 servings

Old-Fashioned Split Pea Soup

- 4 **quarts chicken broth**
- 2 **pounds dried split peas**
- 1 **cup chopped ham**
- ½ **cup chopped onion**
- ½ **cup chopped celery**
- 2 **teaspoons salt**
- 2 **teaspoons black pepper**

1. Place all ingredients in **CROCK-POT®** slow cooker. Stir well to combine. Cover; cook on LOW 8 to 10 hours or on HIGH 4 to 6 hours or until peas are soft.

2. Mix with hand mixer or hand blender on low speed until smooth.

Makes 8 servings

Scalloped Potatoes & Ham

Slow-Cooked Pork & Sauerkraut

2 jars (32 ounces each) sauerkraut, drained and rinsed

1 envelope (1 ounce) dry onion soup mix

3 tablespoons brown mustard

2½ cups water

3 pounds boneless pork loin roast

Combine sauerkraut, soup mix, mustard and water in large mixing bowl. Mix well, then add with pork to **CROCK-POT®** slow cooker. Cover; cook on LOW 8 hours.

Makes 6 servings

Easy Pork Chop Dinner

1 large onion, thinly sliced

3 to 4 medium baking potatoes, sliced

6 pork chops

1 can (10¾ ounces) condensed reduced-fat cream of celery soup, undiluted

½ cup water or milk

1. Place onion and potatoes in **CROCK-POT®** slow cooker. Top with pork chops.

2. Combine soup and water in small bowl; pour over chops. Cover; cook on LOW 6 to 8 hours.

Makes 6 servings

Tip: Serve with salad or vegetables for a delicious dinner.

Slow-Cooked Pork & Sauerkraut

Chorizo Chili

1 pound ground beef

8 ounces raw chorizo sausage, removed from casings

1 can (16 ounces) chili beans in chili sauce

2 cans (14½ ounces each) zesty chili-style diced tomatoes, undrained

1. Place beef and chorizo in **CROCK-POT®** slow cooker. Stir to break up well.

2. Stir in beans and tomatoes. Cover; cook on LOW 7 hours. Skim off and discard excess fat before serving.

Makes 6 servings

Serving Suggestion: Top with sour cream or shredded cheese.

Simply Delicious Pork

1½ pounds boneless pork loin, cut into 6 pieces *or* 6 boneless pork loin chops

4 medium Golden Delicious apples, sliced

3 tablespoons packed brown sugar

1 teaspoon ground cinnamon

½ teaspoon salt

1. Place pork in **CROCK-POT®** slow cooker; cover with apples.

2. Combine brown sugar, cinnamon and salt in small bowl; sprinkle over apples. Cover; cook on LOW 6 to 8 hours.

Makes 6 servings

Chorizo Chili

Chicken & Turkey

Creamy Chicken

3 boneless, skinless chicken breasts *or* 6 boneless, skinless chicken thighs
2 cans (10¾ ounces each) condensed cream of chicken soup, undiluted
1 can (14½ ounces) chicken broth
1 can (4 ounces) sliced mushrooms, drained
½ medium onion, diced
Salt and black pepper
Hot cooked pasta (optional)

Place all ingredients except salt and pepper in **CROCK-POT®** slow cooker. Cover and cook on LOW 6 to 8 hours. Season to taste with salt and pepper. Serve over pasta, if desired.

Makes 3 servings

Tip: If desired, you may add 8 ounces of cubed pasteurized processed cheese spread before serving.

Spicy Turkey with Citrus au Jus

1 bone-in turkey breast, thawed, rinsed and patted dry (about 4 pounds)

4 tablespoons (½ stick) butter, at room temperature

Grated peel of 1 medium lemon

1 teaspoon chili powder

¼ to ½ teaspoon black pepper

⅛ to ¼ teaspoon red pepper flakes

1 tablespoon lemon juice

Salt and black pepper

1. Coat **CROCK-POT®** slow cooker with nonstick cooking spray. Add turkey breast.

2. Mix butter, lemon peel, chili powder, black pepper and pepper flakes in small bowl until well blended. Spread mixture over top and sides of turkey. Cover; cook on LOW 4 to 5 hours or on HIGH 2½ to 3 hours or until meat thermometer reaches 165°F and juices run clear. Do not overcook.

3. Transfer turkey to large cutting board. Let stand 10 minutes before slicing. Turn **CROCK-POT®** slow cooker to LOW.

4. Stir lemon juice into cooking liquid. Pour mixture through fine-mesh sieve; discard solids in sieve. Let mixture stand 5 minutes. Skim and discard excess fat. Add salt and pepper, if desired. Return au jus mixture to **CROCK-POT®** slow cooker. Cover to keep warm. Serve au jus with turkey.

Makes 6 to 8 servings

Slow Cooker Chicken and Dressing

4 **boneless, skinless chicken breasts**
  Salt and black pepper
4 **slices Swiss cheese**
1 **can (14½ ounces) chicken broth**
2 **cans (10¾ ounces each) condensed cream of chicken,**
  celery or mushroom soup, undiluted
3 **cups packaged stuffing mix**
½ **cup (1 stick) butter, melted**

1. Place chicken in **CROCK-POT®** slow cooker. Season with salt and pepper.

2. Top each breast with cheese slice. Add broth and soup. Sprinkle stuffing mix over top; pour melted butter over all. Cover; cook on LOW 6 to 8 hours or on HIGH 3 to 4 hours.

Makes 4 servings

Chicken Sausage Pilaf

1 **pound chicken or turkey sausage, casings removed**
1 **cup uncooked rice and vermicelli pasta mix**
4 **cups chicken broth**
2 **stalks celery, diced**
¼ **cup slivered almonds**
  Salt and black pepper

1. Brown sausage in large skillet over medium-high heat, stirring to break up meat. Drain fat. Add rice and pasta mix to skillet. Cook and stir 1 minute.

2. Place mixture in **CROCK-POT®** slow cooker. Add broth, celery, almonds, salt and pepper to **CROCK-POT®** slow cooker; mix well.

3. Cover; cook on LOW 7 to 10 hours or on HIGH 3 to 4 hours or until rice is tender.

Makes 4 servings

Slow Cooker Chicken and Dressing

Slow Cooker Chicken Dinner

4 boneless, skinless chicken breasts
1 can (10¾ ounces) condensed cream of chicken soup, undiluted
⅓ cup milk
1 package (6 ounces) stuffing mix
1⅔ cups water

Place chicken in **CROCK-POT®** slow cooker. Combine soup and milk in small bowl; mix well. Pour soup mixture over chicken. Combine stuffing mix and water. Spoon stuffing over chicken. Cover; cook on LOW 6 to 8 hours.

Makes 4 servings

Cheesy Slow Cooker Chicken

6 boneless, skinless chicken breasts (about 1½ pounds)
Salt and black pepper
Garlic powder
2 cans (10¾ ounces each) condensed cream of chicken soup, undiluted
1 can (10¾ ounces) condensed Cheddar cheese soup, undiluted
Chopped fresh parsley (optional)

1. Place 3 chicken breasts in **CROCK-POT®** slow cooker. Sprinkle with salt, pepper and garlic powder. Repeat with remaining 3 breasts and seasonings.

2. Combine soups in medium bowl; pour over chicken. Cover; cook on LOW 6 to 8 hours or until chicken is tender. Garnish with parsley, if desired.

Makes 6 servings

Serving Suggestion: The sauce is wonderful over pasta, rice or mashed potatoes.

Slow Cooker Chicken Dinner

Herbed Turkey Breast with Orange Sauce

1 **large onion, chopped**
3 **cloves garlic, minced**
1 **teaspoon dried rosemary**
½ **teaspoon black pepper**
1 **boneless, skinless turkey breast (3 pounds)**
1½ **cups orange juice**

1. Place onion in **CROCK-POT®** slow cooker. Combine garlic, rosemary and pepper in small bowl; set aside. Cut slices about three-fourths of the way through turkey at 2-inch intervals. Rub garlic mixture between slices.

2. Place turkey, cut side up, in **CROCK-POT®** slow cooker. Pour orange juice over turkey. Cover; cook on LOW 7 to 8 hours.

3. Serve sauce from **CROCK-POT®** slow cooker with sliced turkey.

Makes 6 servings

Spicy Shredded Chicken

6 **boneless, skinless chicken breasts (about 1½ pounds)**
1 **jar (16 ounces) salsa**

Place chicken in **CROCK-POT®** slow cooker. Pour salsa over chicken. Cover; cook on LOW 6 to 8 hours or until chicken is tender and no longer pink in center. Shred chicken with 2 forks before serving.

Makes 6 servings

Serving Suggestion: Serve on warm flour tortillas with taco fixings.

Herbed Turkey Breast with Orange Sauce

Ethnic Recipes

Chili Verde

1 **tablespoon vegetable oil**
1 **to 2 pounds boneless pork chops**
  Sliced carrots (enough to cover bottom of CROCK-POT® slow cooker)
1 **jar (24 ounces) mild salsa verde**
  Chopped onion (optional)

1. Heat oil in large skillet over medium-low heat. Brown pork on both sides. Drain excess fat.

2. Place carrot slices in bottom of **CROCK-POT®** slow cooker. Place pork on top of carrots. Pour salsa over chops. Add onion, if desired. Cover; cook on HIGH 6 to 8 hours.

Makes 4 to 8 servings

Serving Suggestion: If desired, shred the pork and serve it with tortillas.

Corned Beef and Cabbage

1 **head cabbage (1½ pounds), cut into 6 wedges**

1 **bag (4 ounces) baby carrots**

1 **corned beef (3 pounds) with seasoning packet***

1 **quart (4 cups) water**

⅓ **cup prepared mustard**

⅓ **cup honey**

*If seasoning packet is not perforated, poke several small holes with tip of paring knife.

1. Place cabbage in **CROCK-POT®** slow cooker; top with carrots. Place seasoning packet on top of vegetables. Place corned beef, fat side up, over seasoning packet and vegetables. Add water. Cover; cook on LOW 10 hours.

2. Combine mustard and honey in small bowl.

3. Discard seasoning packet. Slice beef and serve with vegetables and mustard sauce.

Makes 6 servings

Hot & Sour Chicken

4 **to 6 boneless, skinless chicken breasts (1 to 1½ pounds)**

1 **cup chicken or vegetable broth**

1 **envelope (1 ounce) dry hot-and-sour soup mix**

Place chicken in **CROCK-POT®** slow cooker. Add broth and soup mix. Cover; cook on LOW 5 to 6 hours. Garnish as desired.

Makes 4 to 6 servings

Serving Suggestion: For a nutritious and colorful variation from traditional steamed white rice, serve this dish over a bed of snow peas and sugar snap peas tossed with diced red bell pepper.

Corned Beef and Cabbage

Carne Rellenos

1 **can (4 ounces) whole green chiles, drained**
4 **ounces cream cheese, softened**
1 **flank steak (about 2 pounds)**
1½ **cups salsa verde**

1. Slit whole chiles open on one side with sharp knife; stuff with cream cheese.

2. Open steak flat on sheet of waxed paper; score steak and turn over. Lay stuffed chiles across unscored side of steak. Roll up and tie with kitchen string.

3. Place steak in **CROCK-POT**® slow cooker; pour in salsa. Cover; cook on LOW 6 to 8 hours or on HIGH 3 to 4 hours or until done.

4. Remove steak and cut into 6 pieces. Serve with sauce.

Makes 6 servings

Polska Kielbasa with Beer & Onions

⅓ **cup honey mustard**
⅓ **cup packed dark brown sugar**
18 **ounces brown ale or beer**
2 **kielbasa sausages (16 ounces each), cut into 4-inch pieces**
2 **onions, quartered**

Combine honey mustard and brown sugar in **CROCK-POT**® slow cooker. Whisk in ale. Add sausage pieces. Top with onions. Cover; cook on LOW 4 to 5 hours, stirring occasionally.

Makes 6 to 8 servings

Carne Rellenos

Super-Easy Beef Burritos

 1 **boneless beef chuck roast (2 to 3 pounds)**
 1 **can (28 ounces) enchilada sauce**
    Water (optional)
 4 **(8-inch) flour tortillas**

1. Place roast in **CROCK-POT®** slow cooker; cover with enchilada sauce. Add 2 to 3 tablespoons water, if desired.

2. Cover; cook on LOW 6 to 8 hours or until beef begins to fall apart. Shred beef; serve in tortillas.

Makes 4 servings

Serving Suggestion: Excellent garnishes include shredded cheese, sour cream, salsa, lettuce and tomatoes.

Easy Beef Stroganoff

 3 **cans (10¾ ounces each) condensed cream of mushroom soup, undiluted**
 1 **cup sour cream**
 ½ **cup water**
 1 **envelope (1 ounce) dry onion soup mix**
 2 **pounds beef stew meat**

Combine soup, sour cream, water and onion soup mix in **CROCK-POT®** slow cooker. Add beef; stir until well coated. Cover; cook on LOW 6 hours or on HIGH 3 hours.

Makes 4 to 6 servings

Serving Suggestion: Serve this beef over hot cooked wild rice or noodles along with a salad and grilled bread.

Super-Easy Beef Burritos

Asian Beef with Broccoli

1½ **pounds boneless chuck steak, about 1½ inches thick, sliced thin***

1 **can (10½ ounces) beef consommé**

½ **cup oyster sauce**

2 **tablespoons cornstarch**

1 **bag (16 ounces) fresh broccoli florets**

Hot cooked rice (optional)

Sesame seeds (optional)

*To make slicing steak easier, place in freezer for 30 minutes before slicing.

1. Place steak in **CROCK-POT®** slow cooker. Pour consommé and oyster sauce over meat. Cover; cook on HIGH 3 hours.

2. Combine cornstarch and 2 tablespoons cooking liquid in a cup. Add to **CROCK-POT®** slow cooker. Stir well to combine. Cover; cook 15 minutes longer or until thickened.

3. Poke holes in broccoli bag with fork. Microwave on HIGH (100%) 3 minutes. Empty bag into **CROCK-POT®** slow cooker. Gently toss beef and broccoli together. Serve over cooked rice and garnish with sesame seeds, if desired.

Makes 4 to 6 servings

Mango Ginger Pork Roast

1 **pork shoulder roast (about 4 pounds)**

½ **to 1 teaspoon ground ginger, or to taste**

Salt and black pepper

2 **cups mango salsa**

2 **tablespoons honey**

¼ **cup apricot preserves**

Hot cooked rice (optional)

1. Season roast with ginger, salt and pepper to taste. Transfer to **CROCK-POT®** slow cooker.

2. Combine salsa, honey and preserves. Pour over roast. Cover; cook on LOW 6 to 8 hours. Turn **CROCK-POT®** slow cooker to HIGH and cook 3 to 4 hours longer or until roast is tender. Serve over rice, if desired.

Makes 4 to 6 servings

Sandy's Mexican Chicken

2 **to 4 chicken breasts**

1 **medium onion, sliced**

1 **can (10¾ ounces) condensed cream of chicken soup, undiluted**

1 **can (10 ounces) Mexican-style diced tomatoes with green chiles, undrained**

1 **package (8 ounces) pasteurized process cheese spread, cubed**

1. Place chicken, onion, soup, and tomatoes with chiles in **CROCK-POT®** slow cooker. Cover; cook on LOW 6 to 8 hours or on HIGH 4 hours.

2. Break up chicken into pieces. Add cheese spread; cook on HIGH until melted.

Makes 2 to 4 servings

Serving Suggestion: Serve over hot cooked spaghetti.

Mile-High Enchilada Pie

8 **(6-inch) corn tortillas**

1 **jar (12 ounces) salsa**

1 **can (15½ ounces) kidney beans, drained and rinsed**

1 **cup shredded cooked chicken**

1 **cup (4 ounces) shredded Monterey Jack cheese with jalapeño peppers**
Fresh cilantro and sliced red pepper (optional)

1. Prepare foil handles;* place in **CROCK-POT®** slow cooker. Place 1 tortilla on top of foil handles. Top with small amount of salsa, beans, chicken and cheese. Continue layering in order using remaining ingredients, ending with tortilla and cheese.

2. Cover; cook on LOW 6 to 8 hours or on HIGH 3 to 4 hours. Pull out by foil handles. Garnish with fresh cilantro and sliced red pepper, if desired.

Makes 4 to 6 servings

*To make foil handles, tear off three (18 × 2-inch) strips of heavy foil or use regular foil folded to double thickness. Crisscross foil strips in spoke design and place in **CROCK-POT®** slow cooker to make lifting tortilla stack easier.

Sandy's Mexican Chicken

Sides in a Snap

Barley with Currants and Pine Nuts

- 1 **tablespoon unsalted butter**
- 1 **small onion, finely chopped**
- ½ **cup pearl barley**
- 2 **cups chicken or vegetable broth**
- ½ **teaspoon salt, or to taste**
- ¼ **teaspoon black pepper**
- ⅓ **cup currants**
- ¼ **cup pine nuts**

1. Melt butter in small skillet over medium-high heat. Add onion. Cook and stir until lightly browned, about 2 minutes. Transfer to 1½- to 2-quart **CROCK-POT®** slow cooker. Add barley, broth, salt and pepper. Stir in currants. Cover; cook on LOW 3 hours.

2. Stir in pine nuts and serve immediately.

Makes 4 servings

Cheesy Corn and Peppers

2 **pounds frozen corn kernels**

2 **tablespoons butter, cubed**

2 **poblano chile peppers, chopped** *or* **1 large green bell pepper and 1 jalapeño pepper, seeded and finely chopped***

1 **teaspoon salt**

½ **teaspoon ground cumin**

¼ **teaspoon black pepper**

3 **ounces cream cheese, cubed**

1 **cup (4 ounces) shredded sharp Cheddar cheese**

Chile peppers can sting and irritate the skin; wear rubber gloves when handling peppers and do not touch eyes. Wash hands after handling.

Coat **CROCK-POT®** slow cooker with nonstick cooking spray. Add all ingredients except cream cheese and Cheddar cheese. Cover. Cook on HIGH 2 hours. Add cheeses; stir to blend. Cover. Cook 15 minutes more or until cheeses melt.

Makes 8 servings

Easy Dirty Rice

½ **pound bulk Italian sausage**

2 **cups water**

1 **cup uncooked long grain rice**

1 **large onion, finely chopped**

1 **large green bell pepper, finely chopped**

½ **cup finely chopped celery**

1½ **teaspoons salt**

½ **teaspoon ground red pepper**

½ **cup chopped fresh parsley (optional)**

1. Brown sausage in skillet 6 to 8 minutes over medium-high heat, stirring to break up meat. Drain fat. Place sausage in **CROCK-POT®** slow cooker.

2. Stir in all remaining ingredients except parsley. Cover; cook on LOW 2 hours. Stir in parsley, if desired.

Makes 4 servings

Parmesan Potato Wedges

   2 **pounds red potatoes, cut into ½-inch wedges**
  ¼ **cup finely chopped yellow onion**
  1½ **teaspoons dried oregano**
  ½ **teaspoon salt**
     Black pepper to taste
   2 **tablespoons butter, cut into ⅛-inch pieces**
  ¼ **cup (1 ounce) grated Parmesan cheese**

Layer potatoes, onion, oregano, salt, pepper and butter in **CROCK-POT®** slow cooker. Cover; cook on HIGH 4 hours. Transfer potatoes to serving platter and sprinkle with cheese.

Makes 6 servings

Rustic Garlic Mashed Potatoes

   2 **pounds baking potatoes, unpeeled and cut into ½-inch cubes**
  ¼ **cup water**
   2 **tablespoons butter, cut into ⅛-inch pieces**
  1¼ **teaspoons salt**
  ½ **teaspoon garlic powder**
  ¼ **teaspoon black pepper**
   1 **cup milk**

Place all ingredients except milk in **CROCK-POT®** slow cooker; toss to combine. Cover; cook on LOW 7 hours or on HIGH 4 hours. Add milk to potatoes. Mash potatoes with potato masher or electric mixer until smooth.

Makes 5 servings

Parmesan Potato Wedges

Pesto Rice and Beans

    1 **can (15 ounces) Great Northern beans, rinsed and drained**
    1 **can (14 ounces) chicken or vegetable broth**
  ³/₄ **cup uncooked long-grain white rice**
 1½ **cups frozen cut green beans, thawed and drained**
  ½ **cup prepared pesto**
      Grated Parmesan cheese (optional)

1. Combine Great Northern beans, broth and rice in **CROCK-POT**® slow cooker. Cover; cook on LOW 2 hours.

2. Stir in green beans; cover and cook 1 hour more or until rice and beans are tender.

3. Turn off **CROCK-POT**® slow cooker and remove insert to heatproof surface. Stir in pesto and Parmesan cheese, if desired. Let stand, covered, 5 minutes or until cheese is melted. Serve immediately.

Makes 8 servings

Orange-Spice Glazed Carrots

    1 **package (32 ounces) baby carrots**
  ½ **cup packed light brown sugar**
  ½ **cup orange juice**
    3 **tablespoons butter or margarine**
  ³/₄ **teaspoon ground cinnamon**
  ¼ **teaspoon ground nutmeg**
  ¼ **cup cold water**
    2 **tablespoons cornstarch**

1. Combine carrots, brown sugar, orange juice, butter, cinnamon and nutmeg in 1½- to 3-quart **CROCK-POT**® slow cooker. Cover; cook on LOW 3½ to 4 hours or until carrots are crisp-tender.

2. Spoon carrots into serving bowl. Transfer juices to small saucepan. Bring to a boil.

3. Mix water and cornstarch in cup or small bowl until smooth; stir into saucepan. Boil 1 minute or until thickened, stirring constantly. Spoon over carrots.

Makes 6 servings

Pesto Rice and Beans

Garden Potato Casserole

1¼ **pounds baking potatoes, unpeeled, sliced**

1 **small green or red bell pepper, thinly sliced**

¼ **cup finely chopped yellow onion**

2 **tablespoons butter, cut into pieces, divided**

½ **teaspoon salt**

½ **teaspoon dried thyme leaves**

Black pepper to taste

1 **small yellow squash, thinly sliced**

1 **cup (4 ounces) shredded sharp Cheddar cheese**

1. Place potatoes, bell pepper, onion, 1 tablespoon butter, salt, thyme and black pepper in **CROCK-POT®** slow cooker; mix well. Evenly layer squash over potato mixture; add remaining 1 tablespoon butter.

2. Cover; cook on LOW 7 hours or on HIGH 4 hours.

3. Remove potato mixture to serving bowl. Sprinkle with cheese; let stand 2 to 3 minutes or until cheese melts.

Makes 5 servings

Spinach Gorgonzola Cornbread

2 boxes (8½ ounces each) cornbread mix

3 eggs

½ cup cream

1 box (10 ounces) frozen chopped spinach, thawed and drained

1 cup Gorgonzola crumbles

1 teaspoon black pepper

Paprika (optional)

Mix all ingredients except paprika in medium bowl. Spray inside of 1½- to 2½-quart **CROCK-POT®** slow cooker with nonstick cooking spray. Pour batter into **CROCK-POT®** slow cooker; cover and cook 1½ hours on HIGH. Sprinkle top with paprika for more colorful crust, if desired.

Makes 10 to 12 servings

Note: Cook only on HIGH setting for proper crust and texture.

Sweet-Spiced Sweet Potatoes

2 pounds sweet potatoes, peeled and cut into ½-inch pieces

¼ cup packed dark brown sugar

1 teaspoon ground cinnamon

½ teaspoon ground nutmeg

⅛ teaspoon salt

2 tablespoons butter, cut into ⅛-inch pieces

1 teaspoon vanilla

Combine sweet potatoes, brown sugar, cinnamon, nutmeg and salt in **CROCK-POT®** slow cooker; mix well. Cover; cook on LOW 7 hours or on HIGH 4 hours. Add butter and vanilla; gently stir to blend.

Makes 4 servings

Chicken

TABLE OF CONTENTS

Savory Starters

Stuffed Baby Bell Peppers

  1 **tablespoon extra-virgin olive oil**
 ½ **medium onion, chopped**
 ½ **pound ground chicken**
 ½ **cup cooked white rice**
  1 **tablespoon dry dill weed**
  3 **tablespoons fresh parsley, chopped**
  1 **tablespoon tomato paste, divided**
  2 **tablespoons lemon juice**
 ⅛ **teaspoon black pepper**
 ½ **teaspoon salt**
  1 **bag yellow and red baby bell peppers (16 to 18 peppers)**
 ¼ **cup vegetable, chicken or beef broth**

1. Heat oil in medium skillet over medium heat. Add onion and cook, stirring, 2 minutes or until onion is translucent. Add ground meat and cook, stirring, 8 to 10 minutes or until thoroughly browned. Transfer meat to bowl. Mix in rice, dill, parsley, ½ tablespoon tomato paste, lemon juice, pepper and salt. Mix well.

2. Using paring knife, make slit in side of each pepper and run under cold water to remove any small seeds. Spoon 2 to 3 teaspoons meat mixture into each pepper.

3. In **CROCK-POT®** slow cooker, whisk together broth and remaining ½ tablespoon tomato paste. Arrange peppers in broth, slit side up. Cover and cook on LOW 5 hours.

Makes 16 to 18 servings

Chicken Croustade

 2 **tablespoons canola oil**

1½ **pounds boneless, skinless chicken breasts, chopped into ¼-inch pieces**

 Salt and black pepper

 1 **shallot, minced**

 ¼ **cup white wine**

 1 **large portobello mushroom cap, chopped into ¼-inch pieces**

 1 **tablespoon fresh thyme**

 ¼ **teaspoon sweet paprika**

 ¼ **teaspoon cumin**

 ¼ **cup chicken broth**

 1 **package (6 shells) puff pastry shells** *or* ½ **package (1 sheet) puff pastry dough***

 1 **egg yolk**

 2 **tablespoons cream**

 3 **tablespoons freshly grated Parmesan cheese**

 Minced chives, for garnish

If using puff pastry sheets, thaw, then slice each sheet into 9 squares; bake according to package directions.

1. Heat oil in large skillet over medium heat. Season chicken with salt and pepper and add to skillet. Brown chicken about 4 minutes; do not stir. Turn and brown other side. Place chicken in **CROCK-POT®** slow cooker.

2. Return skillet to low heat and add shallot. Cook 1 minute until shallot softens. Add white wine. Stir to scrape up any brown bits. Cook liquid down to 2 tablespoons then add shallot mixture to **CROCK-POT®** slow cooker. Stir in mushroom, thyme, paprika, cumin, broth, salt and pepper; mix well. Cover and cook on LOW 3 hours.

3. With 1 hour left in cooking time, bake pastry shells according to package directions.

4. With 20 minutes left in cooking time, beat egg yolk and cream together. Add 1 tablespoon cooking liquid from chicken, beating constantly. Whisk mixture into **CROCK-POT®** slow cooker. Cook uncovered on LOW remaining 20 minutes. Stir in Parmesan. Serve chicken filling over puff pastry; garnish with chives.

Makes 6 to 9 servings

Chicken Liver Pâté

1½ **pounds chicken livers, trimmed of fat and membrane**
1 **small onion, thinly sliced**
3 **sprigs fresh thyme**
2 **cloves garlic, peeled and lightly smashed**
¼ **teaspoon salt**
3 **tablespoons cold butter, cut into 4 pieces**
2 **tablespoons heavy cream**
2 **tablespoons sherry**
½ **shallot, minced**
2 **tablespoons fresh parsley, minced**
1 **tablespoon sherry vinegar**
⅛ **teaspoon sugar**
   Salt and black pepper
   Melba toast crackers or toast points, for serving

1. Rinse chicken livers and pat dry. Place in **CROCK-POT®** slow cooker. Add onion, thyme, garlic and ¼ teaspoon salt. Add 1 tablespoon water, cover and cook on LOW 1½ hours.

2. Remove thyme sprigs and discard. Place chicken liver mixture in food processor and pulse to create coarse paste. Add butter pieces one at a time, pulsing to combine. Add cream and sherry and pulse until combined. Transfer mixture to bowl to serve immediately, or place in a small loaf pan and cover with plastic wrap, pressing wrap directly against surface of pâté. Refrigerate overnight until set.

3. Mix shallot, parsley, vinegar, sugar, salt and pepper and let sit for 2 to 3 minutes. Spread on top of pâté. Serve with Melba crackers or toast points.

Makes 8 to 10 servings

Moroccan Spiced Chicken Wings

- ¼ **cup orange juice**
- 3 **tablespoons tomato paste**
- 2 **teaspoons ground cumin**
- 1 **teaspoon curry powder**
- 1 **teaspoon ground turmeric**
- ½ **teaspoon ground cinnamon**
- ½ **teaspoon ground ginger**
- 1 **teaspoon salt**
- 1 **tablespoon olive oil**
- 5 **pounds chicken wings, tips removed and split at joint**

In **CROCK-POT®** slow cooker, combine juice, tomato paste, cumin, curry, turmeric, cinnamon, ginger and salt. Heat oil in large nonstick skillet over medium-high heat. Add wings and brown in several batches, about 6 minutes per batch. Transfer wings to **CROCK-POT®** slow cooker. Toss well to coat with sauce. Cover and cook on HIGH 3 to 3½ hours or until tender.

Makes 8 servings

Oriental Chicken Wings

- 32 **pieces chicken wing drums and flats**
- 1 **cup chopped red onion**
- 1 **cup soy sauce**
- ¾ **cup packed light brown sugar**
- ¼ **cup dry cooking sherry**
- 2 **tablespoons chopped fresh ginger**
- 2 **cloves garlic, minced**
  Chopped fresh chives (optional)

1. Preheat broiler. Broil chicken wing pieces about 5 minutes per side; transfer to **CROCK-POT®** slow cooker.

2. Combine onion, soy sauce, brown sugar, sherry, ginger and garlic in large bowl. Add to **CROCK-POT®** slow cooker; stir to blend well.

3. Cover and cook on LOW 5 to 6 hours or on HIGH 2 to 3 hours. Sprinkle with chives, if desired.

Makes 32 appetizers

Moroccan Spiced Chicken Wings

Asian Lettuce Wraps

  2 **teaspoons canola oil**

1½ **pounds chicken breasts or pork butt, chopped into ¼-inch pieces**

  2 **leeks, chopped into ¼-inch pieces (both white and green parts)**

  1 **cup shiitake mushrooms, stems removed and caps chopped into ¼-inch pieces**

  1 **stalk celery, chopped into ¼-inch pieces**

  1 **teaspoon toasted sesame oil***

  1 **tablespoon oyster sauce***

  1 **tablespoon soy sauce**

  ¼ **teaspoon black pepper**

  2 **tablespoons water**

  1 **bag (8 ounces) cole slaw or broccoli slaw mix**

  ½ **red bell pepper, seeded and cut into thin strips**

  ½ **pound shrimp, shelled, deveined and cut into ¼-inch pieces**

  3 **tablespoons salted, dry roasted peanuts, lightly crushed**

 10 **to 15 leaves crisp romaine lettuce**

     Hoisin sauce*

Available in the Asian foods aisle of your local market.

1. Heat canola oil in small skillet over high heat. Add meat; cook and stir 4 to 5 minutes or until lightly browned on all sides. Transfer to **CROCK-POT®** slow cooker. Add leeks, mushrooms and celery. Stir in sesame oil, oyster sauce, soy sauce, pepper and water. Combine cole slaw and red pepper slices. Layer on top of meat mixture. Cover and cook on LOW 4 hours for chicken, 5 hours for pork.

2. With 20 minutes remaining in cooking time, stir in shrimp. When shrimp are cooked through, turn off heat and stir in crushed peanuts.

3. Wash lettuce leaves and pat dry. Remove white ribs. To serve wraps, spread hoisin sauce as desired on lettuce leaf. Spoon 1 to 2 tablespoons chicken mixture into leaf and roll up like a cigar.

Makes 10 to 15 wraps

Thai Coconut Chicken Meatballs

- 1 **pound ground chicken**
- 2 **green onions, chopped (both white and green parts)**
- 1 **clove garlic, minced**
- 2 **teaspoons toasted sesame oil**
- 1 **teaspoon fish sauce***
- 2 **teaspoons mirin (Japanese rice wine)***
- 1 **tablespoon canola oil**
- ½ **cup coconut milk**
- ¼ **cup chicken broth**
- 1 **teaspoon Thai red curry paste***
- 2 **teaspoons brown sugar**
- 2 **teaspoons lime juice**
- 1 **tablespoon cornstarch**
- 2 **tablespoons cold water**

Available in the Asian foods aisle of your local market.

1. In large bowl, combine chicken, green onions, garlic, sesame oil, fish sauce and mirin. Mix well with hands and form into 1½-inch meatballs.

2. Heat canola oil in skillet over medium heat. Add meatballs and cook, stirring until lightly browned. Alternatively, place meatballs on a cookie sheet and spray with cooking spray. Broil in oven until lightly browned.

3. Place meatballs in **CROCK-POT®** slow cooker. Add coconut milk, chicken broth, curry paste and sugar. Cover and cook on HIGH 3½ to 4 hours.

4. Add lime juice and mix well. In small bowl, whisk together cornstarch and cold water, stirring until it has consistency of heavy cream. Add to **CROCK-POT®** slow cooker. Cook, uncovered on HIGH 10 to 15 minutes longer or until sauce is thick enough to coat meatballs.

Makes 12 to 15 meatballs

Stews & Chilies

Black and White Chili

- 1 **pound chicken tenders, cut into ¾-inch pieces**
- 1 **cup coarsely chopped onion**
- 1 **can (about 15 ounces) Great Northern beans, drained**
- 1 **can (about 15 ounces) black beans, drained**
- 1 **can (about 14 ounces) Mexican-style stewed tomatoes, undrained**
- 2 **tablespoons Texas-style chili powder seasoning mix**

1. Spray large skillet with cooking spray; heat over medium heat until hot. Add chicken and onion; cook and stir 5 minutes or until chicken is browned.

2. Combine chicken mixture, beans, tomatoes with juice and chili seasoning in **CROCK-POT®** slow cooker. Cover; cook on LOW 4 to 4½ hours.

Makes 6 servings

Serving Suggestion: For a change of pace, this delicious chili is excellent served over cooked rice or pasta.

Chinese Chicken Stew

1 **pound boneless, skinless chicken thighs, cut into 1-inch pieces**

1 **teaspoon Chinese five-spice powder***

1/2 **to** 3/4 **teaspoon red pepper flakes**

1 **tablespoon peanut or vegetable oil**

1 **large onion, coarsely chopped**

1 **package (8 ounces) mushrooms, sliced**

2 **cloves garlic, minced**

1 **can (about 14 ounces) chicken broth, divided**

1 **tablespoon cornstarch**

1 **large red bell pepper, cut into** 3/4**-inch pieces**

2 **tablespoons soy sauce**

2 **large green onions, cut into** 1/2**-inch pieces**

1 **tablespoon sesame oil**

3 **cups hot cooked rice (optional)**

1/4 **cup coarsely chopped fresh cilantro (optional)**

Chinese five-spice powder is a blend of cinnamon, cloves, fennel seed, anise and Szechuan peppercorns. It is available in most supermarkets and at Asian grocery stores.

1. Toss chicken with five-spice powder and red pepper flakes in small bowl. Heat peanut oil in large skillet. Add onion and chicken; cook and stir about 5 minutes or until chicken is browned. Add mushrooms and garlic; cook and stir until chicken is no longer pink.

2. Combine 1/4 cup broth and cornstarch in small bowl; set aside. Place cooked chicken mixture, remaining broth, bell pepper and soy sauce in **CROCK-POT®** slow cooker. Cover; cook on LOW 3 1/2 hours or until peppers are tender.

3. Stir in cornstarch mixture, green onions and sesame oil. Cook 30 to 45 minutes or until thickened. Ladle into soup bowls; scoop 1/2 cup rice into each bowl and sprinkle with cilantro, if desired.

Makes 6 servings (about 5 cups)

Chipotle Chicken Stew

1 pound boneless, skinless chicken thighs, cut into cubes

1 can (15 ounces) navy beans, drained and rinsed

1 can (15 ounces) black beans, drained and rinsed

1 can (14½ ounces) crushed tomatoes, undrained

1½ cups chicken broth

½ cup orange juice

1 medium onion, diced

1 chipotle pepper in adobo sauce, minced

1 teaspoon salt

1 teaspoon ground cumin

1 bay leaf

Cilantro sprigs (optional)

1. Combine chicken, beans, tomatoes with juice, broth, orange juice, onion, chipotle pepper, salt, cumin and bay leaf in **CROCK-POT®** slow cooker.

2. Cover; cook on LOW 7 to 8 hours or on HIGH 3½ to 4 hours. Remove bay leaf before serving. Garnish with cilantro sprigs, if desired.

Makes 6 servings

Quatro Frijoles con Pollo Cantaro

1   **cup pitted black olives, drained**

1   **pound boneless, skinless chicken breasts, cubed***

1   **can (16 ounces) garbanzo beans, drained and rinsed**

1   **can (16 ounces) Great Northern or navy beans, drained and rinsed**

1   **can (15 ounces) cannellini beans, drained and rinsed**

1   **can (16 ounces) red kidney beans, drained and rinsed**

1   **can (7 ounces) chopped mild green chiles, drained**

2   **cups chicken stock, plus extra as needed**

2   **tablespoons canola or olive oil**

1   **cup minced onions**

2   **teaspoons minced garlic**

1½ **teaspoons ground cumin**

    Hot sauce, to taste

    Salt and black pepper, to taste

2   **cups crushed corn chips**

6   **ounces Monterey Jack cheese, grated**

Turkey, pork or beef can be substituted for chicken.

1. Combine olives, chicken, beans, chiles and chicken stock in **CROCK-POT®** slow cooker. Mix well; set aside.

2. Heat oil in large skillet over medium-high heat. Cook onion, garlic and cumin until onions are soft, stirring frequently. Add to chicken mixture. Cover; cook on LOW 4 to 5 hours. Check liquid about halfway through, adding more hot broth as needed.

3. Taste and add hot sauce, salt and pepper. Serve in warm bowls and garnish with corn chips and cheese.

Makes 6 servings

Chicken and Chile Pepper Stew

1 **pound boneless, skinless chicken thighs, cut into ½-inch pieces**

1 **pound small potatoes, cut lengthwise into halves, then crosswise into slices**

1 **cup chopped onion**

2 **poblano chile peppers, seeded and cut into ½-inch pieces***

1 **jalapeño pepper, seeded and finely chopped***

3 **cloves garlic, minced**

3 **cups chicken broth**

1 **can (about 14 ounces) diced tomatoes**

2 **tablespoons chili powder**

1 **teaspoon dried oregano**

Chile peppers can sting and irritate the skin, so wear rubber gloves when handling peppers and do not touch your eyes.

1. Place chicken, potatoes, onion, poblano peppers, jalapeño pepper and garlic in **CROCK-POT®** slow cooker.

2. Stir together broth, tomatoes, chili powder and oregano in large bowl. Pour broth mixture over chicken mixture in **CROCK-POT®** slow cooker; mix well. Cover; cook on LOW 8 to 9 hours.

Makes 6 servings

Chicken and Black Bean Chili

1 pound boneless, skinless chicken thighs, cut into 1-inch chunks

2 teaspoons chili powder

2 teaspoons ground cumin

¾ teaspoon salt

1 green bell pepper, diced

1 small onion, chopped

3 cloves garlic, minced

1 can (about 14 ounces) diced tomatoes, undrained

1 cup chunky salsa

1 can (about 15 ounces) black beans, drained and rinsed

Optional toppings: sour cream, diced ripe avocado, shredded Cheddar cheese, sliced green onions or chopped cilantro and/or crushed tortilla or corn chips (optional)

1. Combine chicken, chili powder, cumin and salt in **CROCK-POT®** slow cooker; toss to coat.

2. Add bell pepper, onion and garlic; mix well. Stir in tomatoes and salsa. Cover; cook on LOW 5 to 6 hours or on HIGH 2½ to 3 hours or until chicken is tender.

3. Increase heat to HIGH; stir in beans. Cover; cook 5 to 10 minutes or until beans are heated through. Ladle into bowls; serve with desired toppings.

Makes 4 servings

Impress Your Guests

Chicken Tangier

- **2 tablespoons dried oregano**
- **2 teaspoons seasoning salt**
- **2 teaspoons puréed garlic**
- **¼ teaspoon black pepper**
- **3 pounds skinless chicken thighs**
- **8 thin slices lemon**
- **½ cup dry white wine**
- **2 tablespoons olive oil**
- **1 cup pitted prunes**
- **¼ cup currants or raisins**
- **½ cup pitted green olives**
- **2 tablespoons capers**
- **Hot cooked noodles or rice**
- **Chopped fresh parsley or cilantro, to garnish**

1. Stir together oregano, salt, garlic and pepper in small bowl. Rub mixture onto chicken, coating on all sides.

2. Spray inside of **CROCK-POT®** slow cooker with cooking spray and add chicken. Tuck lemon slices between chicken pieces. Pour wine over chicken and sprinkle olive oil on top. Add prunes, currants, olives and capers. Cover and cook on LOW 7 to 8 hours or on HIGH 4 to 5 hours.

3. To serve, spoon over cooked noodles or rice and sprinkle with chopped fresh parsley or cilantro.

Makes 8 servings

Stuffed Chicken Breasts

- **6 boneless, skinless chicken breasts**
- **8 ounces feta cheese, crumbled**
- **3 cups chopped fresh spinach leaves**
- **⅓ cup oil-packed sun-dried tomatoes, drained and chopped**
- **1 teaspoon minced lemon peel**
- **1 teaspoon dried basil, oregano or mint**
- **½ teaspoon garlic powder**
- **Freshly ground black pepper, to taste**
- **1 can (15 ounces) diced tomatoes, undrained**
- **½ cup oil-cured olives***
- **Hot cooked polenta**

*If using pitted olives, add to **CROCK-POT®** slow cooker in the final hour of cooking.*

1. Place 1 chicken breast between 2 pieces of plastic wrap. Using tenderizer mallet or back of skillet, pound breast until about ¼-inch thick. Repeat with remaining chicken.

2. Combine feta, spinach, sun-dried tomatoes, lemon peel, basil, garlic powder and pepper in medium bowl.

3. Lay pounded chicken, smooth side down, on work surface. Place about 2 tablespoons feta mixture on wide end of breast. Roll tightly. Repeat with remaining chicken.

4. Place rolled chicken, seam side down, in **CROCK-POT®** slow cooker. Top with diced tomatoes with juice and olives. Cover; cook on LOW 5½ to 6 hours or on HIGH 4 hours. Serve with polenta.

Makes 6 servings

Forty-Clove Chicken

    1 **cut-up whole chicken (about 3 pounds)**
       Salt and black pepper
    1 **to 2 tablespoons olive oil**
  ¼   **cup dry white wine**
    2 **tablespoons chopped fresh parsley *or* 2 teaspoons dried parsley flakes**
    2 **tablespoons dry vermouth**
    2 **teaspoons dried basil**
    1 **teaspoon dried oregano**
       Pinch red pepper flakes
  40   **cloves garlic (about 2 heads), peeled***
    4 **stalks celery, sliced**
       Juice and peel of 1 lemon
       Fresh herbs

*The whole garlic bulb is called a head.

1. Remove skin from chicken. Sprinkle chicken with salt and pepper. Heat oil in large skillet over medium heat. Add chicken; brown on all sides. Remove to platter.

2. Combine wine, parsley, vermouth, basil, oregano and red pepper flakes in large bowl. Add garlic and celery; coat well. Transfer garlic and celery to **CROCK-POT®** slow cooker with slotted spoon. Add chicken to remaining herb mixture; coat well. Place chicken on top of celery mixture in **CROCK-POT®** slow cooker. Sprinkle lemon juice and peel over chicken. Cover; cook on LOW 6 hours.

3. Sprinkle with fresh herbs before serving.

Makes 4 to 6 servings

Indian-Style Apricot Chicken

6 **chicken thighs, rinsed and patted dry**
¼ **teaspoon salt**
¼ **teaspoon black pepper**
1 **tablespoon vegetable oil**
1 **large onion, chopped**
2 **cloves garlic, minced**
2 **tablespoons grated fresh ginger**
½ **teaspoon ground cinnamon**
⅛ **teaspoon ground allspice**
1 **can (14½ ounces) diced tomatoes, undrained**
1 **cup chicken broth**
1 **package (8 ounces) dried apricots**
1 **pinch saffron threads (optional)**
   Hot basmati rice
2 **tablespoons chopped fresh parsley**

1. Coat **CROCK-POT®** slow cooker with nonstick cooking spray. Season chicken with salt and pepper. Heat oil in large skillet over medium-high heat until hot. Brown chicken on all sides. Transfer to **CROCK-POT®** slow cooker.

2. Add onion to skillet. Cook and stir 3 to 5 minutes or until translucent. Stir in garlic, ginger, cinnamon and allspice. Cook and stir 15 to 30 seconds longer or until mixture is fragrant. Add tomatoes with juice and broth. Cook 2 to 3 minutes or until mixture is heated through. Pour into **CROCK-POT®** slow cooker.

3. Add apricots and saffron, if desired. Cover; cook on LOW 5 to 6 hours or on HIGH 3 to 3½ hours or until chicken is tender. Add salt and pepper, if desired. Serve with basmati rice and garnish with chopped parsley.

Makes 4 to 6 servings

Note: Use skinless chicken thighs, if desired. To skin chicken easily, grasp skin with paper towel and pull away. Repeat with fresh paper towel for each piece of chicken, discarding skins and towels.

Coq au Vin

2 cups frozen pearl onions, thawed

4 slices thick-cut bacon, crisp-cooked and crumbled

1 cup sliced button mushrooms

1 clove garlic, minced

1 teaspoon dried thyme

⅛ teaspoon black pepper

6 boneless, skinless chicken breasts (about 2 pounds)

½ cup dry red wine

¾ cup reduced-sodium chicken broth

¼ cup tomato paste

3 tablespoons all-purpose flour

Hot cooked egg noodles (optional)

1. Layer onions, bacon, mushrooms, garlic, thyme, pepper, chicken, wine and broth in **CROCK-POT®** slow cooker.

2. Cover; cook on LOW 6 to 8 hours.

3. Remove chicken and vegetables; cover and keep warm. Ladle ½ cup cooking liquid into small bowl; cool slightly. Mix reserved liquid, tomato paste and flour until smooth; stir into **CROCK-POT®** slow cooker. Cook; uncovered, on HIGH 15 minutes or until thickened. Serve over hot noodles, if desired.

Makes 6 servings

Cook's Nook: Coq au Vin is a classic French dish that is made with bone-in chicken, salt pork or bacon, brandy, red wine and herbs. The dish originated when farmers needed a way to cook old chickens that could no longer breed. A slow, moist cooking method was needed to tenderize the tough old birds.

Everyday Gourmet

Thai Chicken

- 2½ **pounds chicken pieces**
- 1 **cup hot salsa**
- ¼ **cup peanut butter**
- 2 **tablespoons lime juice**
- 1 **tablespoon soy sauce**
- 1 **teaspoon minced fresh ginger**
- **Cooked white rice, for serving**
- ½ **cup peanuts, chopped**
- 2 **tablespoons chopped fresh cilantro**

1. Place chicken in **CROCK-POT®** slow cooker. In a bowl, mix together salsa, peanut butter, lime juice, soy sauce and ginger. Pour over chicken.

2. Cover; cook on LOW 8 to 9 hours or on HIGH 3 to 4 hours or until done.

3. To serve, place chicken over rice, pour sauce over chicken; sprinkle with peanuts and cilantro.

Makes 6 servings

Cerveza Chicken Enchilada Casserole

　2　**cups water**
　1　**stalk celery, chopped**
　1　**small carrot, peeled and chopped**
　1　**bottle (12 ounces) Mexican beer, divided**
　　　Juice of 1 lime
　1　**teaspoon salt**
1½　**pounds boneless, skinless chicken breasts**
　1　**can (19 ounces) enchilada sauce, divided**
　7　**ounces white corn tortilla chips**
½　**medium onion, chopped**
　3　**cups shredded Cheddar cheese**
　　　Sour cream, sliced olives and cilantro (optional)

1. Heat water, celery, carrot, 1 cup beer, lime juice and salt in saucepan over high heat until boiling. Add chicken breasts; reduce heat to simmer. Cook until chicken is cooked through, about 12 to 14 minutes. Remove; cool and shred into bite-sized pieces.

2. Spoon ½ cup enchilada sauce in bottom of **CROCK-POT®** slow cooker. Place tortilla chips in 1 layer over sauce. Cover with ⅓ shredded chicken. Sprinkle ⅓ chopped onion over chicken. Add 1 cup cheese, spreading evenly. Pour ½ cup enchilada sauce over cheese. Repeat layering process 2 more times, pouring remaining beer over casserole before adding last layer of cheese.

3. Cook on LOW 3½ to 4 hours. Top with sour cream, sliced olives and cilantro, if desired.

Makes 4 to 6 servings

Mediterranean Chicken Breasts and Wild Rice

 1 **pound boneless, skinless chicken breasts, lightly pounded**
   Kosher salt, to taste
   Black pepper, to taste
 1 **cup white and wild rice blend**
10 **cloves garlic, smashed**
½ **cup oil-packed or dry sun-dried tomatoes***
½ **cup capers, drained**
 2 **cups water**
½ **cup fresh-squeezed lemon juice**
¼ **cup extra-virgin olive oil**

If using dry sun-dried tomatoes, soak in boiling water to soften before chopping.

1. Season chicken with salt and black pepper. Place in **CROCK-POT®** slow cooker. Add rice, garlic, tomatoes and capers; stir well.

2. Mix water, lemon juice and oil in small mixing bowl. Pour mixture over rice and chicken. Stir once to coat chicken. Cover; cook on LOW 8 hours.

Makes 4 servings

Autumn Chicken

 1 can (14 ounces) whole artichoke hearts, drained
 1 can (14 ounces) whole mushrooms, divided
12 boneless, skinless chicken breasts
 1 jar (6½ ounces) marinated artichoke hearts, with liquid
¾ cup white wine
½ cup balsamic vinaigrette
   Hot cooked noodles
   Paprika, for garnish (optional)

Spread whole artichokes over bottom of **CROCK-POT®** slow cooker. Top with half the mushrooms. Layer chicken over mushrooms. Add marinated artichoke hearts with liquid. Add remaining mushrooms. Pour in wine and vinaigrette. Cover; cook on LOW 4 to 5 hours. Serve over noodles. Garnish with paprika, if desired.

Makes 10 to 12 servings

Chicken & Rice

 3 cans (10¾ ounces each) condensed cream of chicken soup, undiluted
 2 cups uncooked instant rice
 1 cup water
 1 pound boneless, skinless chicken breasts or chicken breast tenders
½ teaspoon salt
¼ teaspoon paprika
¼ teaspoon black pepper
½ cup diced celery

Combine soup, rice and water in **CROCK-POT®** slow cooker. Add chicken; sprinkle with salt, paprika and pepper. Sprinkle celery over chicken. Cover; cook on LOW 6 to 8 hours or on HIGH 3 to 4 hours.

Makes 4 servings

Autumn Chicken

Chicken in Honey Sauce

 4 to 6 boneless, skinless chicken breasts
  Salt
  Black pepper
 2 cups honey
 1 cup soy sauce
 ½ cup ketchup
 ¼ cup oil
 2 cloves garlic, minced
  Sesame seeds

1. Place chicken in **CROCK-POT®** slow cooker; season with salt and pepper.

2. Combine honey, soy sauce, ketchup, oil and garlic in medium bowl. Pour over chicken. Cover; cook on LOW 6 to 8 hours or on HIGH 3 to 4 hours.

3. Garnish with sesame seeds before serving.

Makes 4 to 6 servings

Chicken Teriyaki

 1 pound boneless, skinless chicken tenders
 1 can (6 ounces) pineapple juice
 ¼ cup soy sauce
 1 tablespoon sugar
 1 tablespoon minced fresh ginger
 1 tablespoon minced garlic
 1 tablespoon vegetable oil
 1 tablespoon molasses
 24 cherry tomatoes (optional)
 2 cups hot cooked rice

Combine all ingredients except rice in **CROCK-POT®** slow cooker. Cover; cook on LOW 2 hours or until chicken is tender. Serve chicken and sauce over rice.

Makes 4 servings

Chicken in Honey Sauce

Cashew Chicken

  6 **boneless, skinless chicken breasts**
1½ **cups cashews**
  1 **cup sliced mushrooms**
  1 **cup sliced celery**
  1 **can (10¾ ounces) condensed cream of mushroom soup, undiluted**
  ¼ **cup chopped green onion**
  2 **tablespoons butter**
1½ **tablespoons soy sauce**
     Hot cooked rice

1. Combine chicken, cashews, mushrooms, celery, soup, green onion, butter and soy sauce in **CROCK-POT®** slow cooker.

2. Cover; cook on LOW 6 to 8 hours or on HIGH 4 to 6 hours or until done. Serve over rice.

Makes 6 servings

Weeknight Winners

Spanish Paella with Chicken and Sausage

- 1 **tablespoon olive oil**
- 2 **pounds chicken thighs**
- 1 **medium onion, chopped**
- 1 **clove garlic, minced**
- 1 **pound hot smoked sausages, sliced**
- 1 **can (14½ ounces) stewed tomatoes**
- 1 **cup Arborio rice**
- 4 **cups chicken broth**
- 1 **pinch saffron (optional)**
- ½ **cup frozen peas, thawed**

1. Heat oil in large skillet over medium-high heat. Brown chicken on all sides and place in **CROCK-POT®** slow cooker.

2. Add onions to skillet, cook and stir until translucent. Stir in garlic, sausages, tomatoes, rice, chicken broth and saffron. Pour mixture over chicken.

3. Cover and cook on HIGH 3 to 4 hours or until chicken and rice are tender. Remove chicken pieces to platter and fluff rice with fork. Stir in peas. Spoon rice onto platter with chicken.

Makes 4 servings

Greek Chicken Pitas with Creamy Mustard Sauce

Filling

- 1 **medium green bell pepper, cored, seeded and sliced into ½-inch strips**
- 1 **medium onion, cut into 8 wedges**
- 1 **pound boneless skinless chicken breasts, rinsed and patted dry**
- 1 **tablespoon extra-virgin olive oil**
- 2 **teaspoons dried Greek seasoning blend**
- ¼ **teaspoon salt**

Sauce

- ¼ **cup plain fat-free yogurt**
- ¼ **cup mayonnaise**
- 1 **tablespoon prepared mustard**
- ¼ **teaspoon salt**
- 4 **whole pita rounds**
- ½ **cup crumbled feta cheese**

  Optional toppings: Sliced cucumbers, sliced tomatoes, Kalamata olives

1. Coat **CROCK-POT®** slow cooker with nonstick cooking spray. Place bell pepper and onion in bottom. Add chicken, and drizzle on oil. Sprinkle evenly with seasoning and ¼ teaspoon salt. Cover; cook on HIGH 1¾ hours or until chicken is no longer pink and vegetables are crisp-tender.

2. Remove chicken and slice. Remove vegetables using slotted spoon.

3. To prepare sauce: Combine yogurt, mayonnaise, mustard and ¼ teaspoon salt in small bowl. Whisk until smooth.

4. Warm pitas according to package directions. Cut in half, and fill with chicken, sauce, vegetables and feta cheese. Top as desired.

Makes 4 servings

Roast Chicken with Peas, Prosciutto and Cream

- 1 **cut-up whole chicken (about 2½ pounds)**
  Salt and black pepper, to taste
- 5 **ounces prosciutto, diced**
- 1 **small white onion, finely chopped**
- ½ **cup dry white wine**
- 1 **package (10 ounces) frozen peas**
- ½ **cup heavy cream**
- 1½ **tablespoons cornstarch**
- 2 **tablespoons water**
- 4 **cups farfalle pasta, cooked al dente**

1. Season chicken pieces with salt and pepper. Combine chicken, prosciutto, onion and wine in **CROCK-POT®** slow cooker. Cover; cook on LOW 8 to 10 hours or on HIGH 3½ to 4 hours until chicken is no longer pink in center.

2. During last 30 minutes of cooking, add frozen peas and heavy cream to cooking liquid.

3. Remove chicken with slotted spoon. Carve meat and set aside on warmed platter.

4. Combine cornstarch and water. Add to cooking liquid in **CROCK-POT®** slow cooker. Cover; cook on HIGH 10 to 15 minutes or until thickened.

5. To serve, spoon pasta onto individual plates. Place chicken on pasta and top each portion with sauce.

Makes 6 servings

Chicken and Spicy Black Bean Tacos

1 **can (15 ounces) black beans, drained and rinsed**
1 **can (10 ounces) tomatoes with mild green chiles, drained**
1½ **teaspoons chili powder**
¾ **teaspoon ground cumin**
1 **tablespoon plus 1 teaspoon extra-virgin olive oil, divided**
12 **ounces boneless, skinless chicken breasts, rinsed and patted dry**
12 **crisp corn taco shells**
   Optional toppings: shredded lettuce, diced tomatoes, shredded cheese, sour cream, ripe olives

1. Coat **CROCK-POT®** slow cooker with nonstick cooking spray. Add beans and tomatoes with chiles. Blend chili powder and cumin with 1 teaspoon oil and rub onto chicken breasts. Place chicken in **CROCK-POT®** slow cooker. Cover; cook on HIGH 1¾ hours.

2. Remove chicken and slice. Transfer bean mixture to bowl using slotted spoon. Stir in 1 tablespoon oil.

3. To serve, warm taco shells according to package directions. Fill with equal amounts of bean mixture and chicken. Add toppings as desired.

Makes 4 servings

Chicken Cacciatore

¼ cup vegetable oil

2½ to 3 pounds chicken tenders, cut into bite-size pieces

1 can (28 ounces) crushed Italian-style tomatoes

2 cans (8 ounces each) Italian-style tomato sauce

1 medium onion, chopped

1 can (4 ounces) sliced mushrooms, drained

2 cloves garlic, minced

1 teaspoon salt

1 teaspoon dried oregano leaves

½ teaspoon dried thyme leaves

½ teaspoon black pepper

Hot cooked spaghetti or rice

1. Heat oil in large skillet over medium-low heat. Brown chicken on all sides. Drain excess fat.

2. Transfer chicken to **CROCK-POT®** slow cooker. Add remaining ingredients except spaghetti. Cover; cook on LOW 6 to 8 hours. Serve over spaghetti.

Makes 6 to 8 servings

Chicken and Mushroom Fettuccine Alfredo

1½ **pounds chicken breast cutlets, rinsed, patted dry and cut into strips**

2 **packages (8 ounces each) cremini mushrooms, cut into thirds**

½ **teaspoon salt**

½ **teaspoon black pepper**

¼ **teaspoon garlic powder**

2 **packages (8 ounces each) cream cheese, cut into pieces**

2 **sticks butter, cut into pieces**

1½ **cups grated Parmesan cheese, plus additional for serving**

1½ **cups whole milk**

1 **box (8 ounces) fettuccine noodles**

1. Coat inside of **CROCK-POT®** slow cooker with nonstick cooking spray. Add chicken strips in single layer. Distribute mushrooms evenly over chicken. Sprinkle salt, pepper and garlic powder over mushrooms.

2. In medium saucepan over medium heat, stir together cream cheese, butter, 1½ cups cheese and milk. Whisk continuously until smooth and heated through. Pour mixture over mushrooms, pushing down any mushrooms that float to top. Cover and cook on LOW 4 to 5 hours.

3. Cook fettuccine according to package directions. Drain. Add fettuccine to **CROCK-POT®** slow cooker and toss gently with sauce. Serve with additional Parmesan cheese.

Makes 6 to 8 servings

Traditional Cassoulet

1 **small onion, finely chopped**

2 **cloves garlic, finely chopped**

½ **cup finely chopped peeled carrots**

½ **cup roughly chopped seeded tomatoes**

1 **can (about 15 ounces) cannellini beans, drained and rinsed**

¼ **cup bread crumbs**

2 **tablespoons finely chopped fresh marjoram**

2 **tablespoons finely chopped fresh parsley**

2 **tablespoons olive oil**

1½ **pounds chicken thighs**

½ **pound bulk pork sausage**

½ **cup dry white wine**

½ **cup chicken broth**

1. Combine onion, garlic, carrots, tomatoes, beans, bread crumbs and fresh herbs in **CROCK-POT®** slow cooker.

2. Heat olive oil in large skillet over medium-high heat. Add chicken in single layer (in batches, if necessary) and cook 3 to 4 minutes per side or until brown. Place chicken on top of mixture in **CROCK-POT®** slow cooker. Add sausage to skillet. Cook, stirring to break up meat, until cooked through. Transfer sausage to **CROCK-POT®** slow cooker with slotted spoon.

3. Return skillet to medium-high heat. Add wine and chicken broth to skillet and stir to scrape up any browned bits. Bring to a boil and cook until liquid is reduced to about one third its original volume. Remove from heat.

4. Pour reduced liquid over contents of **CROCK-POT®** slow cooker. Cover and cook on LOW 6 to 7 hours or on HIGH 3½ hours.

Makes 4 servings

Soups & Stews

TABLE OF CONTENTS

Family Favorites

Curried Sweet Potato and Carrot Soup

 2 medium-to-large sweet potatoes, peeled and cut into ¾-inch dice (about 5 cups)
 2 cups baby carrots
 1 small onion, chopped
 ¾ teaspoon curry powder
 ½ teaspoon salt, or to taste
 ½ teaspoon black pepper
 ½ teaspoon ground cinnamon
 ¼ teaspoon ground ginger
 4 cups chicken broth
 1 tablespoon maple syrup
 ¾ cup half-and-half
   Candied ginger (optional)

1. Place sweet potatoes, carrots, onion, curry powder, salt, pepper, cinnamon and ginger in **CROCK-POT®** slow cooker. Add chicken broth. Stir well to combine. Cover; cook on LOW 7 to 8 hours.

2. Pureé soup, 1 cup at a time, in blender, returning soup to **CROCK-POT®** slow cooker after each batch. (Or, use immersion blender.) Add maple syrup and half-and-half. Add salt and pepper, if desired. Cover; cook on HIGH 15 minutes to reheat. Serve in bowls and garnish with strips or pieces of candied ginger.

Makes 8 servings

Double Corn Chowder

2 small celery stalks, trimmed and chopped

6 ounces Canadian bacon, chopped

1 small onion or 1 large shallot, chopped

1 serrano chile or jalapeño pepper, cored, seeded and minced*

1 cup frozen corn, thawed

1 cup canned hominy

¼ teaspoon salt, or to taste

¼ teaspoon crushed dried thyme

¼ teaspoon black pepper, or to taste

1 cup chicken broth

1 tablespoon all-purpose flour

1½ cups milk, divided**

*Hot peppers can sting and irritate the skin, so wear rubber gloves when handling peppers and do not touch your eyes.

**For richer chowder, use ¾ cup milk and ¾ cup half-and-half.

1. Combine celery, Canadian bacon, onion, chile pepper, corn, hominy, salt, thyme and pepper in **CROCK-POT®** slow cooker. Add broth. Cover; cook on LOW 5 to 6 hours or on HIGH 3 to 3½ hours.

2. Turn **CROCK-POT®** slow cooker to LOW. Stir together flour and 2 tablespoons milk in small bowl. Stir into corn mixture. Add remaining milk. Cover; cook on LOW 20 minutes.

Makes 4 servings

Penne Pasta Zuppa

1 **can (15 ounces) white beans, drained and rinsed**
2 **medium yellow squash, diced**
2 **ripe tomatoes, diced**
2 **small red potatoes, cubed**
2 **leeks, sliced into quarters lengthwise then chopped**
1 **carrot, peeled and diced**
¼ **pound fresh green beans, washed, stemmed and diced**
2 **fresh sage leaves, minced**
1 **teaspoon salt**
½ **teaspoon black pepper**
8 **cups water**
¼ **pound uncooked penne pasta**
   Grated Romano cheese (optional)

1. Combine beans, squash, tomatoes, potatoes, leeks, carrot, green beans, sage, salt and pepper in **CROCK-POT**® slow cooker. Add water. Stir well to combine. Cover; cook on HIGH 2 hours, stirring occasionally. Turn **CROCK-POT**® slow cooker to LOW. Cook, covered, 8 hours longer. Stir occasionally.

2. Turn **CROCK-POT**® slow cooker to HIGH. Add pasta. Cover; cook 30 minutes longer or until pasta is done.

3. To serve, garnish with Romano cheese, if desired.

Makes 6 servings

Manhattan Clam Chowder

  3 **slices bacon, diced**
  2 **stalks celery, chopped**
  3 **onions, chopped**
  2 **cups water**
  1 **can (15 ounces) stewed tomatoes, undrained and chopped**
  4 **small red potatoes, diced**
  2 **carrots, diced**
  ½ **teaspoon dried thyme**
  ½ **teaspoon black pepper**
  ½ **teaspoon Louisiana-style hot sauce**
  1 **pound minced clams***

If fresh clams are unavailable, use canned clams; 6 (6½-ounce) cans yield about 1 pound of clam meat; drain and discard liquid.

1. Cook and stir bacon in medium saucepan until crisp. Remove bacon and place in **CROCK-POT®** slow cooker.

2. Add celery and onions to skillet. Cook and stir until tender. Place in **CROCK-POT®** slow cooker.

3. Mix in water, tomatoes with juice, potatoes, carrots, thyme, pepper and hot sauce. Cover; cook on LOW 6 to 8 hours or HIGH 4 to 6 hours. Add clams during last half hour of cooking.

Makes 4 servings

Tip: Shellfish and bivalves are delicate and should be added to the **CROCK-POT®** slow cooker during the last 15 to 30 minutes of the cooking time if you're using the HIGH heat setting, and during the last 30 to 45 minutes if you're using the LOW setting. This type of seafood overcooks easily, becoming tough and rubbery, so watch your cooking times, and cook only long enough for foods to be done.

Potato Cheddar Soup

    2 pounds red-skin potatoes, peeled and cut into 1/2-inch cubes
   3/4 cup coarsely chopped carrots
    1 medium onion, coarsely chopped
    3 cups chicken broth
   1/2 teaspoon salt
    1 cup half-and-half
   1/4 teaspoon black pepper
    2 cups (8 ounces) shredded Cheddar cheese

1. Place potatoes, carrots, onion, broth and salt in **CROCK-POT®** slow cooker. Cover; cook on LOW 6 to 7 hours or on HIGH 3 to 3½ hours or until vegetables are tender.

2. Stir in half-and-half and pepper. Cover; cook on HIGH 15 minutes. Turn off heat and remove cover; let stand 5 minutes. Stir in cheese until melted.

Makes 6 servings

Cauliflower Soup

    2 heads cauliflower, cut into small florets
    8 cups chicken broth
   3/4 cup chopped celery
   3/4 cup chopped onion
    2 teaspoons salt
    2 teaspoons black pepper
    2 cups milk or light cream
    1 teaspoon Worcestershire sauce

1. Combine cauliflower, broth, celery, onion, salt and pepper in **CROCK-POT®** slow cooker. Cover; cook on LOW 7 to 8 hours or on HIGH 3 to 4 hours.

2. Using a hand mixer or hand blender, purée soup until smooth. Mix in milk and Worcestershire sauce, continuing to blend until smooth. Cook on HIGH 15 to 20 minutes longer before serving.

Makes 8 servings

Potato Cheddar Soup

Granny's Apple Cidered Onion Soup with Gouda Cinnamon Toast

2 tablespoons olive oil

4 tablespoons butter, cubed, divided

4 medium to large onions, peeled and thinly sliced

2 medium Granny Smith apples, peeled, cored and chopped

4 cups chicken broth

1½ cups apple cider

2 tablespoons brandy (optional)

Salt and freshly ground black pepper, to taste

6 slices French or Italian bread, cut about ½ inch thick

2 tablespoons sugar

½ teaspoon ground cinnamon

2 cups shredded Gouda cheese, preferably aged

1. Spoon oil over bottom of **CROCK-POT®** slow cooker; add 2 tablespoons butter, distributing evenly. Add onions and apples. Cover; cook on LOW 8 to 10 hours or until onions are softened and caramelized.

2. Add broth, cider and brandy, if desired. Season with salt and black pepper. Cover; cook on HIGH about 1 hour or until hot.

3. While soup is heating, make Gouda Cinnamon Toast: Preheat broiler. Spread remaining 2 tablespoons softened butter on one side of bread slices. Combine sugar and cinnamon. Sprinkle evenly over buttered bread. Place bread on baking sheet and toast under broiler until golden brown.

4. Remove from oven; turn bread over and sprinkle untoasted side with Gouda cheese. Return to broiler until cheese melts, taking care not to burn.

5. To serve, ladle soup into bowls and float 1 piece Gouda Cinnamon Toast on top of each serving, cheese side up. Serve immediately.

Makes 6 servings

Celery-Leek Bisque

3 bunches leeks (about 3 pounds), trimmed*

2 medium stalks celery, sliced

1 medium carrot, peeled and sliced

3 cloves garlic, minced

2 cans (about 14 ounces each) fat-free chicken broth

1 package (8 ounces) cream cheese with garlic and herbs

2 cups half-and-half, plus more for garnish

Salt and black pepper

Fresh basil leaves (optional)

*It is very important to rinse leeks thoroughly before using. The gritty sand in which leeks are grown can become trapped between the layers of leaves and can be difficult to see. Cut trimmed leeks in half lengthwise and submerge in several inches of cool water several times to rinse off any trapped sand.

1. Combine leeks, celery, carrots, garlic and broth in **CROCK-POT®** slow cooker. Cover and cook on LOW 8 hours or on HIGH 4 hours.

2. Purée until smooth in blender, 1 cup at a time, returning batches to **CROCK-POT®** slow cooker as they are processed. Add cream cheese to last batch in blender and purée until smooth; stir cream cheese mixture and 2 cups half-and-half into soup. Add salt and pepper to taste. Serve immediately, or cool to room temperature and refrigerate in airtight container (flavors intensify overnight). Reheat before serving. Garnish with additional half-and-half and basil leaves, if desired.

Makes 4 to 6 servings

Flavors of the World

Niku Jaga (Japanese Beef Stew)

- 2 **tablespoons vegetable oil**
- 2 **pounds beef stew meat, cut in 1-inch cubes**
- 4 **medium carrots, peeled and sliced diagonally**
- 3 **medium Yukon Gold potatoes, peeled and chopped**
- 1 **white onion, peeled and chopped**
- 1 **cup water**
- ½ **cup Japanese sake** *or* ½ **cup dry white wine**
- ¼ **cup sugar**
- ¼ **cup soy sauce**
- 1 **teaspoon salt**

1. Heat oil in skillet over medium heat until hot. Sear beef on all sides, turning as it browns. Transfer beef to **CROCK-POT**® slow cooker. Add remaining ingredients. Stir well to combine.

2. Cover; cook on LOW 10 to 12 hours or on HIGH 4 to 6 hours.

Makes 6 to 8 servings

Mediterranean Shrimp Soup

2 cans (14½ ounces each) fat-free reduced-sodium chicken broth

1 can (14½ ounces) diced tomatoes

1 can (8 ounces) tomato sauce

1 medium onion, chopped

½ medium green bell pepper, chopped

½ cup orange juice

½ cup dry white wine (optional)

1 jar (2½ ounces) sliced mushrooms

¼ cup sliced pitted black olives

2 cloves garlic, minced

1 teaspoon dried basil

2 bay leaves

¼ teaspoon whole fennel seeds, crushed

⅛ teaspoon black pepper

1 pound medium raw shrimp, peeled and deveined

1. Place all ingredients except shrimp in **CROCK-POT®** slow cooker. Cover; cook on LOW 4 to 4½ hours or until vegetables are crisp-tender.

2. Stir in shrimp. Cover; cook 15 to 30 minutes or until shrimp are pink and opaque. Remove and discard bay leaves.

Makes 6 servings

Note: For a heartier soup, add 1 pound of firm white fish (such as cod or haddock), cut into 1-inch pieces, 45 minutes before end of cooking time.

French Lentil Rice Soup

6 cups chicken broth or vegetable broth

1 cup lentils, picked over and rinsed

2 medium carrots, peeled and finely diced

1 small onion, finely chopped

2 stalks celery, finely diced

3 tablespoons uncooked white rice

2 tablespoons minced garlic

1 teaspoon herbes de Provence *or* **1 teaspoon dried thyme**

½ teaspoon salt

⅛ teaspoon ground white pepper*

¼ cup heavy cream *or* **¼ cup sour cream, divided (optional)**

¼ cup chopped parsley (optional)

*Substitute black pepper, if desired.

1. Stir together broth, lentils, carrots, onion, celery, rice, garlic, herbes de Provence, salt and pepper in **CROCK-POT®** slow cooker. Cover and cook on LOW 8 hours or on HIGH 4 to 5 hours.

2. Remove 1½ cups soup and purée in food processor or blender until almost smooth.** Stir puréed soup back into **CROCK-POT®** slow cooker.

3. Divide soup evenly among four serving bowls garnishing each with 1 tablespoon cream and 1 tablespoon chopped parsley, if desired.

Makes 4 servings

**Use caution when processing hot liquids in blender. Vent lid of blender and cover with clean kitchen towel as directed by manufacturer.

Tuscany Bean and Prosciutto Soup

2 **tablespoons unsalted butter**

4 **slices prosciutto***

3 **cups water**

1 **cup dried navy beans, rinsed and sorted**

½ **cup dried lima beans, rinsed and sorted**

1 **medium yellow onion, finely chopped**

1 **tablespoon chopped fresh cilantro**

1 **teaspoon salt**

1 **teaspoon ground cumin**

1 **teaspoon black pepper**

½ **teaspoon ground paprika**

2 **cans (15 ounces each) diced tomatoes, undrained**

Substitute 4 slices bacon, if desired.

1. Melt butter in large skillet over medium-high heat. Add prosciutto and fry until crisp. Remove to paper towels to cool.

2. Crumble prosciutto into small pieces in **CROCK-POT®** slow cooker. Add water, navy beans, lima beans, onion, cilantro, salt, cumin, black pepper and paprika. Stir well to combine. Cover and cook on LOW 10 to 12 hours.

3. Turn **CROCK-POT®** slow cooker to HIGH. Add tomatoes and juice and stir well. Cover and cook on HIGH 30 to 40 minutes or until soup is heated through.

Makes 6 servings

Greek Lemon and Rice Soup

3 cans (about 14 ounces each) chicken broth

½ cup long-grain white rice (not converted or instant rice)

3 egg yolks

¼ cup fresh lemon juice

¼ teaspoon salt

⅛ teaspoon ground white pepper*

4 thin slices lemon (optional)

4 teaspoons finely chopped parsley (optional)

Substitute black pepper if desired.

1. Stir chicken broth and rice together in **CROCK-POT®** slow cooker. Cover and cook on HIGH 2 to 3 hours or until rice is cooked.

2. Turn **CROCK-POT®** slow cooker to LOW. Whisk egg yolks and lemon juice together in medium bowl. Whisk large spoonful of hot rice mixture into egg yolk mixture. Whisk back into **CROCK-POT®** slow cooker.

3. Cook on LOW 10 minutes. Season with salt and pepper. Ladle soup into serving bowls and garnish each bowl with thin slice of lemon and 1 teaspoon chopped parsley, if desired.

Makes 4 servings

Note: Soup may be served hot or cold. To serve cold, allow soup to cool to room temperature. Cover and refrigerate up to 24 hours before serving.

Italian Hillside Garden Soup

1 **tablespoon extra-virgin olive oil**

1 **cup chopped green bell pepper**

1 **cup chopped onion**

½ **cup sliced celery**

1 **can (about 14 ounces) diced tomatoes with basil, garlic and oregano, undrained**

1 **can (15½ ounces) navy beans, drained and rinsed**

1 **medium zucchini, chopped**

1 **cup frozen cut green beans, thawed**

2 **cans (about 14 ounces each) chicken broth**

¼ **teaspoon garlic powder**

1 **package (9 ounces) refrigerated sausage- and cheese-filled tortellini pasta**

3 **tablespoons chopped fresh basil**

Grated Asiago or Parmesan cheese (optional)

1. Heat oil in large skillet over medium-high heat. Add bell pepper, onion and celery; cook and stir 4 minutes or until onions are translucent. Remove mixture to **CROCK-POT®** slow cooker.

2. Add tomatoes with juice, navy beans, zucchini, green beans, broth and garlic powder. Cover; cook on LOW 7 hours or on HIGH 3½ hours.

3. Turn **CROCK-POT®** slow cooker to HIGH. Stir in tortellini. Cover; cook on HIGH 20 to 25 minutes or until pasta is tender. Stir in basil. Garnish each serving with cheese.

Makes 6 servings

Tip: Cooking times are guidelines. **CROCK-POT®** slow cookers, just like ovens, cook differently depending on a variety of factors, including capacity. For example, cooking times will be longer at high altitudes.

Fresh Lime and Black Bean Soup

2 cans (15 ounces each) black beans, undrained
1 can (14½ ounces) reduced-sodium chicken broth
1½ cups chopped onion
1½ teaspoons chili powder
¾ teaspoon ground cumin
¼ teaspoon garlic powder
⅛ to ¼ teaspoon red pepper flakes
½ cup sour cream
2 tablespoons extra-virgin olive oil
2 tablespoons chopped cilantro
1 medium lime, cut into wedges

1. Coat **CROCK-POT®** slow cooker with nonstick cooking spray. Add beans, broth, onion, chili powder, cumin, garlic powder and pepper flakes. Cover; cook on LOW 7 hours or on HIGH 3½ hours, or until onions are very soft.

2. Process 1 cup soup mixture in blender until smooth and return to **CROCK-POT®** slow cooker. Stir, check consistency, and repeat with additional 1 cup soup, as needed to achieve desired consistency. Let stand 15 to 20 minutes before serving.

3. Ladle soup into 4 bowls. Divide sour cream, oil and cilantro evenly among servings. Squeeze juice from lime wedge over each.

Makes 4 servings

Tip: Brighten the flavor of dishes cooked in the **CROCK-POT®** slow cooker by adding fresh herbs or fresh lemon or lime juice just before serving.

Dinner in a Bowl

Hearty Mushroom and Barley Soup

- 9 **cups chicken broth**
- 1 **package (16 ounces) sliced fresh button mushrooms**
- 1 **large onion, chopped**
- 2 **carrots, chopped**
- 2 **stalks celery, chopped**
- ½ **cup uncooked pearl barley**
- ½ **ounce dried porcini mushrooms**
- 3 **cloves garlic, minced**
- 1 **teaspoon salt**
- ½ **teaspoon dried thyme**
- ½ **teaspoon black pepper**

Combine all ingredients in **CROCK-POT®** slow cooker; stir until well blended. Cover; cook on LOW 4 to 6 hours.

Makes 8 to 10 servings

Variation: For even more flavor, add a beef or ham bone to the **CROCK-POT®** slow cooker with the rest of the ingredients.

Hearty Meatball Stew

3 pounds ground beef or ground turkey

1 cup Italian bread crumbs

4 eggs

½ cup milk

¼ cup grated Romano cheese

2 teaspoons salt

2 teaspoons garlic salt

2 teaspoons black pepper

2 tablespoons olive oil

2 cups water

2 cups beef broth

1 can (14½ ounces) stewed tomatoes, undrained

1 can (12 ounces) tomato paste

1 cup chopped carrots

1 cup chopped onions

¼ cup chopped celery

1 tablespoon Italian seasoning

1. Combine beef, bread crumbs, eggs, milk, cheese, salt, garlic salt and pepper in large bowl. Form into 2-inch-round balls. Heat oil in skillet over medium-high heat until hot. Brown meatballs on all sides. Transfer to **CROCK-POT®** slow cooker.

2. Add remaining ingredients. Stir well to combine. Cover; cook on LOW 4 to 6 hours or on HIGH 2 to 4 hours.

Makes 6 to 8 servings

My Mother's Sausage and Vegetable Soup

  1 **can (15 ounces) black beans, drained and rinsed**
  1 **can (about 14 ounces) diced tomatoes**
  1 **can (10¾ ounces) condensed cream of mushroom soup, undiluted**
  ½ **pound smoked turkey sausage, cut into ½-inch slices**
  2 **cups diced potato**
  1 **cup chopped onion**
  1 **cup chopped red bell pepper**
  ½ **cup water**
  2 **teaspoons extra-hot prepared horseradish**
  2 **teaspoons honey**
  1 **teaspoon dried basil**

Combine all ingredients in **CROCK-POT®** slow cooker, mix well. Cover; cook on
LOW 7 to 8 hours or until potato is tender.

Makes 6 to 8 servings

Rich and Hearty Drumstick Soup

> 2 turkey drumsticks (about 1¾ pounds total)
> 2 medium carrots, peeled and sliced
> 1 medium stalk celery, thinly sliced
> 1 cup chopped onion
> 1 teaspoon minced garlic
> ½ teaspoon poultry seasoning
> 4½ cups chicken broth
> 2 ounces uncooked dry egg noodles
> ¼ cup chopped parsley
> 2 tablespoons butter
> ¾ teaspoon salt, or to taste

1. Coat **CROCK-POT®** slow cooker with nonstick cooking spray. Add drumsticks, carrots, celery, onion, garlic and poultry seasoning. Pour broth over; cover. Cook on HIGH 5 hours or until turkey meat is falling off bones.

2. Remove turkey; set aside. Add noodles to **CROCK-POT®** slow cooker; cover and cook 30 minutes more or until noodles are tender. Meanwhile, debone turkey and cut meat into bite-size pieces; set meat aside.

3. When noodles are cooked, stir in turkey, parsley, butter and salt.

Makes 4 servings

Beggar's Chowder

¼ **cup unsalted butter, at room temperature**

¼ **cup all-purpose flour**

1 **tablespoon garlic salt**

1 **tablespoon thyme**

1 **tablespoon sweet Hungarian paprika**

½ **teaspoon coarsely ground black pepper**

4 **skinless bone-in turkey legs or thighs, trimmed of visible fat**

2 **cans (14½ ounces each) cream-style sweet corn**

1 **can (10¾ ounces) condensed chicken broth, undiluted**

1½ **cups diced yellow onion**

1 **cup diced red bell pepper**

1 **cup diced green bell pepper**

1 **pound cleaned, stemmed white mushrooms, halved or quartered if large**

1 **can (14½ ounces) petite diced tomatoes, drained**

1½ **cups heavy whipping cream**

½ **cup chopped cilantro or parsley, plus additional for garnish**

Salt and black pepper, to taste

1. Coat **CROCK-POT®** slow cooker with nonstick cooking spray. Combine butter, flour, garlic salt, thyme, paprika and pepper in small bowl. Use back of wooden spoon to work mixture into smooth paste. Rub paste into all sides of turkey.

2. Place turkey in **CROCK-POT®** slow cooker. Add corn, broth, onion and bell peppers.

3. Cover; cook on HIGH 3 hours or until turkey is fork-tender. Remove turkey; set aside until cool enough to handle.

4. Add mushrooms and tomatoes to cooking liquid. Cover; cook on HIGH 30 minutes longer.

5. Meanwhile, remove turkey meat from bones in bite-size pieces. When mushrooms are tender, return turkey to **CROCK-POT®** slow cooker. Add cream and cilantro. Cook, covered, about 15 minutes or until heated through. Add salt and pepper, if desired. Garnish with additional chopped cilantro, if desired.

Makes 8 servings

Hearty Beef Recipes

Mexican Cheese Soup

- **1 pound processed cheese, cubed**
- **1 pound ground beef, cooked and drained**
- **1 can (8¾ ounces) whole kernel corn, undrained**
- **1 can (15 ounces) kidney beans, undrained**
- **1 jalapeño pepper, seeded and diced (optional)***
- **1 can (14½ ounces) diced tomatoes with green chiles, undrained**
- **1 can (14½ ounces) stewed tomatoes, undrained**
- **1 envelope taco seasoning**

Jalapeño peppers can sting and irritate the skin; wear rubber gloves when handling peppers and do not touch eyes. Wash hands after handling.

1. Coat inside of **CROCK-POT®** slow cooker with nonstick cooking spray. Combine cheese, beef, corn, beans with liquid, jalapeño, if desired, tomatoes with chiles, stewed tomatoes and taco seasoning in prepared **CROCK-POT®** slow cooker.

2. Cover; cook on LOW 4 to 5 hours or on HIGH 3 hours or until done.

Makes 6 to 8 servings

Serving Suggestion: Corn chips make an excellent accompaniment to this hearty soup.

Grandma Ruth's Minestrone

1 **pound ground beef**

1 **cup dried red kidney beans**

1 **package (16 ounces) frozen mixed vegetables**

2 **cans (8 ounces each) tomato sauce**

1 **can (about 14 ounces) diced tomatoes, undrained**

¼ **head shredded cabbage**

1 **cup chopped onions**

1 **cup chopped celery**

½ **cup chopped fresh parsley**

1 **tablespoon dried basil**

1 **tablespoon Italian seasoning**

1 **teaspoon salt**

1 **teaspoon black pepper**

1 **cup cooked macaroni**

1. Combine ground beef and beans in **CROCK-POT®** slow cooker. Cover; cook on HIGH 2 hours.

2. Turn **CROCK-POT®** slow cooker to LOW. Add all remaining ingredients except macaroni and stir to blend. Cover; cook on LOW for 6 to 8 hours or until beans are tender.

3. Turn **CROCK-POT®** slow cooker to HIGH. Stir macaroni into **CROCK-POT®** slow cooker. Cover; cook on HIGH for 1 hour.

Makes 4 servings

Hamburger Veggie Soup

1 **pound 95% lean ground beef**

1 **bag (16 ounces) frozen mixed vegetables**

1 **package (10 ounces) frozen seasoning-blend vegetables***

1 **can (10¾ ounces) condensed tomato soup, undiluted**

1 **can (about 14 ounces) stewed tomatoes, undrained**

2 **cans (5½ ounces each) spicy vegetable juice**

   Salt and black pepper, to taste

Seasoning-blend vegetables are a mixture of chopped bell peppers, onions and celery. If you're unable to find frozen vegetables, use ½ cup of each fresh vegetable.

Coat **CROCK-POT®** slow cooker with nonstick cooking spray. Crumble beef before placing in bottom. Add remaining ingredients. Stir well to blend. Cover; cook on HIGH 4 hours. If necessary, break up large pieces of beef. Add salt and pepper before serving, if desired.

Makes 4 to 6 servings

Sweet and Sour Brisket Stew

  1 **jar (12 ounces) chili sauce**

  1½ **to 2 tablespoons packed dark brown sugar**

  1½ **tablespoons fresh lemon juice**

  ¼ **cup beef broth**

  1 **tablespoon Dijon mustard**

  ¼ **teaspoon paprika**

  ½ **teaspoon salt, or to taste**

  ¼ **teaspoon black pepper, or to taste**

  1 **clove garlic, minced**

  1 **small onion, chopped**

  1 **well-trimmed beef brisket, cut into 1-inch pieces***

  2 **large carrots, cut into ½-inch slices**

  1 **tablespoon all-purpose flour (optional)**

*Beef brisket has a heavy layer of fat, which some supermarkets trim off. If the meat is trimmed, buy 2½ pounds; if not, purchase 4 pounds, then trim and discard excess fat.

1. Combine sauce, 1½ tablespoons brown sugar, lemon juice, broth, mustard, paprika, salt and pepper in **CROCK-POT**® slow cooker. (Add remaining sugar, if desired, after tasting.)

2. Add garlic, onion, beef and carrots. Stir well to coat. Cover; cook on LOW 8 hours.

3. If thicker gravy is desired, whisk together 1 tablespoon flour and 3 tablespoons cooking liquid in small bowl. Add to **CROCK-POT**® slow cooker. Cover; cook on HIGH 10 minutes, or until thickened.

Makes 6 to 8 servings

Beef Fajita Soup

1 pound beef stew meat

1 can (15 ounces) pinto beans, drained and rinsed

1 can (15 ounces) black beans, drained and rinsed

1 can (about 14 ounces) diced tomatoes with roasted garlic, undrained

1 can (about 14 ounces) beef broth

1 small green bell pepper, thinly sliced

1 small red bell pepper, thinly sliced

1 small onion, thinly sliced

1½ cups water

2 teaspoons ground cumin

1 teaspoon seasoned salt

1 teaspoon black pepper

Combine beef, beans, tomatoes with juice, broth, bell peppers, onion, water, cumin, salt and black pepper in **CROCK-POT®** slow cooker. Cover; cook on LOW 8 hours.

Makes 8 servings

Serving Suggestion: Serve topped with sour cream, shredded Monterey Jack or Cheddar cheese and chopped olives.

Beef Stew with Molasses and Raisins

⅓ cup all-purpose flour

2 teaspoons salt, divided

1½ teaspoons black pepper, divided

2 pounds beef stew meat, cut into 1½-inch pieces

5 tablespoons oil, divided

2 medium onions, sliced

1 can (28 ounces) diced tomatoes, drained

1 cup beef broth

3 tablespoons molasses

2 tablespoons cider vinegar

4 cloves garlic, minced

2 teaspoons dried thyme

1 teaspoon celery salt

1 bay leaf

8 ounces baby carrots, cut in half lengthwise

2 parsnips, diced

½ cup golden raisins

1. Combine flour, 1½ teaspoons salt and 1 teaspoon pepper in large bowl. Toss meat in flour mixture. Heat 2 tablespoons oil in large skillet or Dutch oven over medium-high heat until hot. Add half of beef and brown on all sides. Set aside browned beef and repeat with 2 additional tablespoons oil and remaining beef.

2. Add remaining 1 tablespoon oil to skillet. Add onions and cook, stirring to loosen any browned bits, about 5 minutes. Add tomatoes, broth, molasses, vinegar, garlic, thyme, celery salt, bay leaf and remaining ½ teaspoon salt and ½ teaspoon pepper. Bring to a boil. Add browned beef and boil 1 minute.

3. Transfer to **CROCK-POT®** slow cooker. Cover; cook on LOW 5 hours or on HIGH 2½ hours. Add carrots, parsnips and raisins. Cook 1 to 2 hours longer or until vegetables are tender. Remove and discard bay leaf.

Makes 6 to 8 servings

Chicken Soups

Hearty Chicken Tequila Soup

- 1 **small onion, cut into 8 wedges**
- 1 **cup frozen corn, thawed**
- 1 **can (14½ ounces) diced tomatoes with mild green chiles, undrained**
- 2 **cloves garlic, minced**
- 2 **tablespoons chopped fresh cilantro, plus additional for garnish**
- 1 **whole chicken (about 3½ pounds)**
- 2 **cups chicken broth**
- 3 **tablespoons tequila**
- ¼ **cup sour cream**

1. Spread onions in bottom of **CROCK-POT®** slow cooker. Add corn, tomatoes with chiles, garlic and 2 tablespoons cilantro. Mix well to combine. Place chicken on top of tomato mixture.

2. Combine broth and tequila in medium bowl. Pour over chicken. Cover; cook on LOW 8 to 10 hours.

3. Transfer chicken to cutting board and let rest until cool enough to handle. Remove skin and bones. Pull meat apart with 2 forks into bite-size pieces. Return chicken to **CROCK-POT®** slow cooker and stir.

4. Serve with dollop of sour cream and garnish with cilantro.

Makes 2 to 4 servings

Chicken & Barley Soup

1 cup thinly sliced celery

1 medium onion, coarsely chopped

1 carrot, cut into thin slices

½ cup medium pearl barley

1 clove garlic, minced

1 cut-up whole chicken (about 3 pounds)

1 tablespoon olive oil

2½ cups chicken broth

1 can (about 14 ounces) diced tomatoes, undrained

¾ teaspoon salt

½ teaspoon dried basil

¼ teaspoon black pepper

1. Place celery, onion, carrot, barley and garlic in **CROCK-POT**® slow cooker.

2. Remove and discard skin from chicken pieces. Separate drumsticks from thighs. Trim back bone from breasts. Save wings for another use. Heat oil in large skillet over medium-high heat; brown chicken pieces on all sides. Place chicken in **CROCK-POT**® slow cooker.

3. Add broth, tomatoes with juice, salt, basil and pepper. Cook on LOW 7 to 8 hours or HIGH 4 hours or until chicken and barley are tender. Remove chicken and debone. Cut chicken into bite-size pieces; stir into soup.

Makes 4 servings

Country Chicken Chowder

2 tablespoons margarine or butter

1½ pounds boneless, skinless chicken breast tenders, cut into ½-inch pieces

2 small onions, chopped

2 stalks celery, sliced

2 small carrots, peeled and sliced

2 cups frozen corn

2 cans (10¾ ounces each) condensed cream of potato soup, undiluted

1½ cups chicken broth

1 teaspoon dried dill weed

½ cup half-and-half

1. Melt margarine in large skillet. Add chicken; cook until browned.

2. Add cooked chicken, onions, celery, carrots, corn, soup, chicken broth and dill to **CROCK-POT®** slow cooker. Cover and cook on LOW 3 to 4 hours or until chicken is no longer pink and vegetables are tender.

3. Turn off heat; stir in half-and-half. Cover and let stand 5 to 10 minutes or just until heated through.

Makes 8 servings

Note: For a special touch, garnish soup with croutons and fresh dill.

Creamy Farmhouse Chicken and Garden Soup

½ **(16-ounce) package frozen pepper stir-fry vegetable mix**

1 **cup frozen corn**

1 **medium zucchini, sliced**

2 **bone-in chicken thighs, skinned**

½ **teaspoon minced garlic**

1 **can (about 14 ounces) fat-free chicken broth**

½ **teaspoon dried thyme**

2 **ounces uncooked egg noodles**

1 **cup half-and-half**

½ **cup frozen green peas, thawed**

2 **tablespoons chopped parsley**

2 **tablespoons butter, melted**

1 **teaspoon salt**

½ **teaspoon coarsely ground black pepper**

1. Coat **CROCK-POT®** slow cooker with nonstick cooking spray. Place stir-fry vegetables, corn and zucchini in bottom. Add chicken, garlic, broth and thyme. Cover; cook on HIGH 3 to 4 hours or until chicken is no longer pink. Remove chicken and set aside to cool slightly.

2. Add noodles to **CROCK-POT®** slow cooker. Cover; cook 20 minutes longer, or until noodles are done.

3. Meanwhile, debone and chop chicken. Return to **CROCK-POT®** slow cooker. Stir in remaining ingredients. Let stand 5 minutes before serving.

Makes 4 servings

Note: To skin chicken easily, grasp skin with paper towel and pull away. Repeat with fresh paper towel for each piece of chicken, discarding skins and towels.

Index

Metric Conversion Chart

VOLUME MEASUREMENTS (dry)

$1/8$ teaspoon = 0.5 mL
$1/4$ teaspoon = 1 mL
$1/2$ teaspoon = 2 mL
$3/4$ teaspoon = 4 mL
1 teaspoon = 5 mL
1 tablespoon = 15 mL
2 tablespoons = 30 mL
$1/4$ cup = 60 mL
$1/3$ cup = 75 mL
$1/2$ cup = 125 mL
$2/3$ cup = 150 mL
$3/4$ cup = 175 mL
1 cup = 250 mL
2 cups = 1 pint = 500 mL
3 cups = 750 mL
4 cups = 1 quart = 1 L

VOLUME MEASUREMENTS (fluid)

1 fluid ounce (2 tablespoons) = 30 mL
4 fluid ounces ($1/2$ cup) = 125 mL
8 fluid ounces (1 cup) = 250 mL
12 fluid ounces ($1 1/2$ cups) = 375 mL
16 fluid ounces (2 cups) = 500 mL

WEIGHTS (mass)

$1/2$ ounce = 15 g
1 ounce = 30 g
3 ounces = 90 g
4 ounces = 120 g
8 ounces = 225 g
10 ounces = 285 g
12 ounces = 360 g
16 ounces = 1 pound = 450 g

DIMENSIONS

$1/16$ inch = 2 mm
$1/8$ inch = 3 mm
$1/4$ inch = 6 mm
$1/2$ inch = 1.5 cm
$3/4$ inch = 2 cm
1 inch = 2.5 cm

OVEN TEMPERATURES

250°F = 120°C
275°F = 140°C
300°F = 150°C
325°F = 160°C
350°F = 180°C
375°F = 190°C
400°F = 200°C
425°F = 220°C
450°F = 230°C

BAKING PAN AND DISH EQUIVALENTS

Utensil	Size in Inches	Size in Centimeters	Volume	Metric Volume
Baking or Cake Pan (square or rectangular)	8×8×2	20×20×5	8 cups	2 L
	9×9×2	23×23×5	10 cups	2.5 L
	13×9×2	33×23×5	12 cups	3 L
Loaf Pan	$8 1/2 × 4 1/2 × 2 1/2$	21×11×6	6 cups	1.5 L
	9×9×3	23×13×7	8 cups	2 L
Round Layer Cake Pan	$8 × 1 1/2$	20×4	4 cups	1 L
	$9 × 1 1/2$	23×4	5 cups	1.25 L
Pie Plate	$8 × 1 1/2$	20×4	4 cups	1 L
	$9 × 1 1/2$	23×4	5 cups	1.25 L
Baking Dish or Casserole			1 quart/4 cups	1 L
			$1 1/2$ quart/6 cups	1.5 L
			2 quart/8 cups	2 L
			3 quart/12 cups	3 L